Greatness

From Ordinary to Extraordinary in Any Part of Your Life

Eric Rios

Managing editor: Alice Sullivan, www.alicesullivan.com

Cover Design by Akivda M – A Creative Digital Design Agency

Published in the United States by REAL Coaching & Consulting Group, LLC

Contents

Dedication

This book is dedicated to my loving wife and children for believing in me as I wrote this book. For my son, Josh, who was constantly asking me when I was going to be done with writing. For my son, Sam, who is my right-hand man in all I do. For my son, Caleb, who is currently serving in the U.S. Army and cannot be home to share in this adventure. And to my beautiful daughters, Faith, Hailey, and Hannah, for putting up with me talking about all of my business adventures with them and their friends. My daughter-in-laws Danielle and Lisa, for being great wives to my boys Sam and Caleb, and setting great examples to follow.

And at last, to my wife, who has been my absolute encouragement through the writing of this book and through all of the hard times being in business. She has been my rock through this last ten years and I just want to say thank you for being a part of this great adventure of creating *greatness* in our lives.

Foreword

As an educator and small business consultant, I am always on the lookout for resources that put all the pieces together in a manageable way, and I believe I have found it in *The Complete Book on Greatness*. As a business teacher, this book will be very useful to me in my development of student leaders and counseling of business owners; it is an effective tool I can use to get them on the right track because it puts it all the effective components together in one place.

So many people in modern society simply give up when obstacles appear in front of them. Not the author of this book, Eric Rios. I have marveled at and been inspired by Eric over the time I have known him. He simply refuses to let unforeseen or even self-inflicted challenges keep him down. Both professionally and in his personal life, Eric sets goals and relentlessly works to achieve them—no matter how long it takes or what resources he needs to access. His recognition of and attention to his self-sabotaging habits and his ability to overcome them is truly remarkable. Eric's quest to find a purposeful life has set him on this amazing course to conquer obstacles personally, professionally, and spiritually. His knack for overcoming so many seemingly impossible situations has given him experience that few have. This experience, coupled with an insatiable appetite to consume every book and recording by all the great motivators, allows us to cut to the chase.

Do not miss out on Eric's words of wisdom. Enjoy his energy and easy-to-understand style. By welcoming Eric's message you can find the clarity you need to move forward, and discover your level of competence in all you aspire to achieve. He will happily guide you through your fears and expose the confidence you need to excel. He will help you find that inner courage you need to commit to finding personal success through easy-to-use steps and tips. Let us appreciate his earned wisdom and his voracious consumption of all things motivational. May we focus on living the life we want.

—Michael Oliva

Introduction

Your life can be exactly what you want it to be, with the right direction. In my own life, I have benefitted from the stories of so many people to help me get to where I am today. Not only have I used their stories for motivation, I have applied the advice I learned from each one of them. I hope my story will do the same for you—encourage and motivate you, while providing some wisdom along the way.

Growing into who I wanted to become—and who I didn't want to remain—has been one of the most challenging things I have personally done. It didn't come easy, or without missteps, obstacles, and frustrations, but the result is worth every bit of discomfort I encountered.

Wild Child

As a child, I lived with my grandparents through most of my early childhood, from when I was around two to around seven years old. They were two of the most amazing role models I could have ever asked for. My grandmother was a strong, brave woman who did not back down from anything that came her way. She was loving and caring, and made her family her number-one priority.

Every Christmas was celebrated at her house, where all of the family came together from both my grandmother's side and my grandfather's side. This was an absolute joyous time for me as a kid because I got lots of presents!

While I was deeply loved, I didn't get away with too much. I remember tricking my grandmother into thinking I was sick by taking warm water and putting it into my mouth before I had her take my temperature. (It worked—so don't tell your kids or they might just try this.) But when I got caught lying, I got the switch.

My grandfather, on the other hand, was a very strong and stern man. He did so much with us grandkids, from taking us hiking and fishing, playing ball with us in the yard, and teaching me how to mow the lawn when I was just seven years old. I would grab the handle of the lawn mower and he would stand behind me and help me push. A hard-working man, my grandfather was a great example of what we should be as we get older.

Having a strong example to follow from both my grandparents was an amazing seed of greatness planted in my life that would eventually grow into something great. Being able to learn from my grandfather's amazing work ethic was the best thing that could have ever happened to me, and I have provided that same work ethic to all of my kids to make sure that when they are grown, they will be willing to work hard themselves.

Growing up in Tulsa, Oklahoma, was fun, though it was not without some disappointments when it came to having a broken family. My mom and dad divorced when I was five, and Ruben, my dad, didn't come around much after that. My brother is thirteen months older than me, so he and I were really close growing up, and my sister is four years older than me, so I was the annoying little brother that drove her and everyone else around me crazy.

When I was eighteen, I heard rumors that someone else might be my father, but it was not verified. Many years later, when I was forty-two, I decided to see if the rumors were true, so I had a DNA test done to see if Ruben was my father. He was the father of my two siblings—but he wasn't *my* father. After asking many questions, I learned my real father had died when he was fifty-three years old from brain cancer.

When Ruben found out I was not his real son, he was devastated and told me that day was the worst day of his life. At that point, I hadn't seen him in over thirty years; he was never around. For me, it was just another day of disappointment. I was never going to have a relationship with my real father, who had already passed away.

My mom married my stepfather, Bob, after her divorce from Ruben, which only lasted seven or eight years. I never had a real father figure, but the one constant in my life as a kid was my grandparents, until my grandfather passed away when I was around fourteen years old. This was really tough for me, as he was the only man I was ever close to. My grandmother moved in with my mom, my brother and sister, and me, and lived with us until she had to move into an assisted living facility.

I didn't ever seem to do well in school, despite the guidance and wishes of my grandparents. They were only able to enforce my good behavior until my mom married my stepfather when I was seven years old. A stubborn kid, I always did what I wanted, no matter what anyone told me. I wasn't dumb; I just didn't want to do any of the schoolwork. I continued to struggle with my grades so much that I flunked the eighth grade and had to do it all over again, and still barely passed the second time around.

During my second stint in the eighth grade, I was tested to see what was wrong with me. I had a college IQ, a lot of energy, and a short attention span. No matter how I was punished or encouraged to do better, I found no value in going to school. I saw schoolteachers as being very biased toward the kids who seemed to be smarter and got the good grades in class. In fact, in all my years in school, I only remember one time when I actually enjoyed myself and felt I learned something. When I was in the fourth grade, I was in a reading class I loved, and for one project I got to be a weatherman on a newscast team. We acted out the whole skit like we were actually on television. I excelled in this class because it gave me the ability to be creative and to be active, instead of sitting in my seat and focusing straight ahead on the chalkboard for an hour.

As an adult I have studied how people learn and how different teaching styles don't always match children's learning styles. When that happens, students end up struggling in school. But back then, there wasn't any research to suggest that students could be taught another way.

After graduating the eighth grade, my family moved away to another state to get a new start and in hopes that I would become better student and grow out of my seemingly rebellious behavior. What I didn't know was that no matter where you go to get a new start, you still have to take *you* with you. No matter where you end up in life, *you* are still going to be there. In an unfamiliar town, the only thing that had changed was my geographical location—not me. I was still the kid who did not care about doing well in school.

After one semester of the ninth grade, I had been suspended five times for trivial things like skipping school. I ended up flunking every class I attended, and this included P.E. and Art. Now, who flunks P.E.? Well, I did, of course. I decided to tell my mom that I was going to drop out of school at the age of fifteen. I know this had to be extremely disappointing to my mom after enduring so many years of me struggling through classes. With some resistance, my mom allowed me to drop out. At this time in our lives, she realized that she had to pick her battles, and she decided that she would not win this one. My sister, on the other hand, had already graduated from school and was living on her own. She was the student who did really well in school and took honor classes. So at least one of us had graduated.

Now what would I do since I was no longer in school? The one thing I did like doing—working. I always liked the idea of making money, and I always saw myself as someone better than what I was, or what others saw. After my mom got divorced from my stepfather, things became really tough financially for us. He was a vice president of a large bank, and my mom was an office manager of a construction company. But the problem with being in construction is how volatile the industry is—one day you could have a job and the next the job is gone. I remember us being broke so many times. Yet my mom was always a great example of someone who worked. Many times she'd work two jobs just so we could eat and have a place to lay our heads at night.

When one construction site closed, my mom took a job working for another construction company and moved from Virginia to California, and my brother and me moved in with my sister and her husband. Ruben lived in another state, and was never around to offer any kind of support. I was seventeen years old and working in fast food. Soon after my mom settled, she asked me if I wanted to come to California to stay with her and I said yes. I took the money I had raised from working and bought myself a bus ticket to California.

After arriving in California, I was still a pretty rowdy kid but nothing like I was when I was younger. I did not have an education to speak of except one semester of the ninth grade. Still, I was able to get a job right away working fast food. Later that year, I was able to get a job working at a cotton gin doing laboring work. It paid more and seemed like more of a "real job" to me.

One night I was lying on the couch watching television, and I saw a commercial about a welding school. I had no idea what welding really was but it looked interesting. So I told my mom that I wanted to go to this school. Because I was not eighteen, I was not able to sign myself up to start school, so she went with me. School was still school to me, and I did not really apply myself as much as I should have, though I did complete the school in nine months and became a certified welder. Though I knew nothing except for the basic skills of welding, I was happy that I now had a trade that I could be a part of.

I took my first *real* job when I was eighteen years old, working in a blacksmith shop in the city of Bakersfield, making a measly five dollars an hour. It wasn't enough money in my mind, but I ended up liking it. Still, having the welding certification didn't guarantee a job. During the early 1990s, the welding industry in California was on a roller coaster ride. The industry was up and down, so you worked when there was work and you were laid off when the work slowed down. I was laid off fourteen times during the next four and half years—being so young, with very little actual work experience, it made me more susceptible to being the first guy laid off.

Amidst all the uncertainty with work, I got married at the ripe old age of eighteen. Living the adult life with no real direction was hard. My marriage lasted seven years and we had three wonderful boys. But with no education and no goals to be anything more than only what I knew—how to be a welder—I was now challenged with making some decisions in my life. Not only did I have the challenge of keeping a job during a horrible market for the welding trade, but I had kids to support as well.

The divorce was very costly and hard on everyone involved. I moved away from California to Texas on a bus with my boys and a suitcase. I got a pretty good job working for a mechanical contractor, learning the trade of plumbing. The pay was not good, but the opportunity was good for moving up and I needed to provide for my kids. I started out making $8.44 an hour as a first-year apprentice. But I had one problem—I still did not have the GED I needed to actually *start* the apprenticeship program. I spent the next six months going to night classes and studying so I could make this happen as quickly as possible.

This was my first time of actually having a real goal that I had to accomplish in a short amount of time. I got my GED in the mail the day I had to turn it in to the school for me to be able to start. I was now enrolled in a school where I would get a great education along with college credits towards the classes I was taking. For me, it was a prayer answered. You see, back when I was seventeen years old, I had given my life to Jesus Christ, and that was when my life and attitude changed for the better.

When I lived in Bakersfield, California, with my mother, I met a great group of people and started going to church with them. One Sunday evening, Pastor Don Burton preached a message about salvation and I found myself going to the altar and giving my life to Christ. It was a small United Pentecostal Church, but one that had life to give a young man who was struggling to find his way. This change in me caused me to start working toward a better lifestyle.

I had some great mentors at this time in the church, and it was perfect timing. My mom ended up having to leave California with her job, so I stayed alone as a young seventeen-year-old kid, going to welding school and working in the cotton gin, until my mom's friend Jean decided to take me in. My friends in Bakersfield—Jean, Eddie, and Loreda, along with Pastor Don Burton—made such an impact in my life. They were what greatness looked like, and they helped teach me about making good choices in my life.

For the first time in many years, I had a male figure in my life that actually cared about my well-being. Jean, Eddie, and Loreda helped me stay on task of completing school and getting a job. Eddie had at times let me work in his tree-trimming business. When he needed help he let me come work with him. Jean, on the other hand, was a great example of perseverance in hardship, as she had gone through a divorce and was raising her two girls Angie and Nancy, who I would sometimes babysit when Jean needed help. Loreda was a go-getter in her life and portrayed a get-it-done kind of attitude that I found very appealing. I created a lasting friendship with these families.

Now back to my current life in Texas. I had taken a job working for a company as a plumbing apprentice and was going to school for an apprenticeship to become a journeyman plumber. At this time, as a single parent to three boys, I met a young lady who lived in the same apartments as me. She had an amazing daughter named Amber, who got along very well with my boys. After some time, we got married and had a daughter together.

Sadly, after seven years, we got divorced. This was a huge challenge for my boys at this time, as they had now found themselves in another broken family. But the one thing they had was a dad who made it his priority to make sure they were loved and cared for.

Once again I found myself divorced—and now with four children to support. Being married was tough for me, as I had no idea what a good marriage looked like, and I had no real idea of what a good husband was supposed to be or do. I saw it modeled in other people's lives but I couldn't quite figure out how to adopt those same behaviors in my own life. One thing about me, I was committed to being married, no matter how screwed up the marriage was. My kids were always my number-one concern when it came to me living the life example in front of them. I kept my kids focused on being busy and playing sports so the struggles of the marriage weren't their struggles too.

I knew that my life had to reflect what I wanted my kids' lives to look like, so I searched my own heart to figure out how I could change as an individual. As I looked deep within myself, I realized that I needed to change who I was first, no matter what. I did not blame my ex-wives for my shortcomings, rather I decided I was going to change and set some new goals to become a new person from within. In my job, I had experienced exactly what it was to have a definite plan based on a definite set of goals. Now I needed to set goals for my personal life.

I decided to write down my first list of goals, which were centered on my behavior and would allow me to become a different person in both my personal life and future married life. I looked at all of my shortcomings that I wanted to change, and recognized that all of our behaviors are based on habits. Some habits being good, and some being bad. I first looked at who I wanted to be as a man and then as a husband. I became clear on who I needed to become to have a more successful life if I was ever to be married again. I made a list so detailed that I knew how I would act, react, and so on when it came to my behavior. For many years I had lived in survival mode and never with a purpose. Now my life had a newfound purpose, and this purpose required that I become great. This first started with me changing my habits.

Along the way, I had accumulated so many self-defeating habits that were destroying my life. Some of these habits were the everyday things that you do on a daily basis that don't really serve you as a human being. It could be as simple as your reactions to a situation, your lack of taking action when you needed to, and so on. I knew for the first time exactly who I wanted to be as a person, and I was determined to become that person. I told myself I would read this list every single day, over and over until my life reflected the new habits I was creating for myself. I read this list starting in the morning and read it at least ten times throughout the day, especially before bed. And I watched my life transform from the inside out. This list of lifestyle changes was for me, but I knew that they would benefit others directly once the new habits were instilled into my DNA.

Once I felt confident that I had changed my behaviors and was seeing progress, I was once again open to a relationship. I was not just shopping for a new woman, but rather I was being very choosy in finding someone. This was not me jumping back into a rebound relationship, but rather me just being a man who loved living life to the fullest. One thing I had learned from being married before was I knew exactly what I wanted in a wife, and what I did not want in a wife. By me knowing what I wanted in a woman, it ended up being easier than I thought to find the right woman.

Shelly met all the requirements I had in a woman. We took it slow and got to know each other before we met each other's kids. We've now been married over ten years, and I can tell you without a doubt this has been the best ten years of my adult life. Now don't get me wrong, there have been challenges—but not with my wife. In the ten years we have been together, we have only gone to bed mad only a couple of times, and that was because I had too much pride to just say, "I'm sorry."

When you know who you want to be in life, it seems that life is so much easier. You are no longer living your life on accident, but instead you are living your life on purpose with intention. You have decided what kind of life you want to live and have made it a priority to live that way. Being married for me now is so much easier because I made sure I found the woman who would help me fulfill my life and help her fulfill hers. We even help each other reach dreams we thought had passed us by.

When I was in my twenties and going to church, I had a great passion of becoming a pastor, but I never did because I saw my life as one that was so messed up in so many ways—like being a twice-divorced single dad of four—that I walked away from that dream. We would all love to have a perfect life with all the circumstances perfect in every way—but that's not reality.

In the kind of church I attended they looked down on divorce, especially if you were going to be in ministry. When I look back at the dream I had of being a pastor, I don't think I ever really gave up on the *dream*, I just saw it as one that would never be attained because of my life's circumstances. Life has been an enormous challenge for me as an adult, but the amazing thing about it is that I am so grateful for all I have gone through in this life because it has made me who I am today. Now, as a successful business owner and a youth pastor, I have realized my dreams of being successful in a career and being in ministry. Through these two areas, I can speak to every person who thought they weren't good enough, or didn't have enough education or enough talent to make something of themselves—and to every kid who has had a tough life, or who comes from a broken home.

Hardships can be great motivators to help you become more in life. Everything takes time, especially when it comes to creating an amazing life. If you will just take the time and decide what kind of life you want, your life can and will be so different. I have personally used all of the principles in this book to design an amazing life.

As you learn about yourself and consider your options, don't judge yourself against someone else's life, but judge your life against what you have *decided you want* out of this life. If you never take the time to decide what kind of life you want to live, then there is only one person to blame—yourself. As you read these pages, apply what you learn throughout this book and make the commitment to yourself to take action based on what you discover.

You have an amazing opportunity to create the best life possible. It's time to start dreaming again and reaching for greatness.

Notes:

"It's a lack of clarity that creates chaos and frustration. Those emotions are poison to any living goal." ~ *Steve Maraboli*

Chapter 1

Clarity

If you don't know, you can't go.

Do you know what the actual definition of what clarity is? Let's start with the Merriam Webster online dictionary definition[1]:

clar·i·ty / ˈklerəti/ noun

a: the quality of being clear: such as a : the quality of being easily understood

b: the quality of being expressed, remembered, understood, etc., in a very exact way

As you read through this chapter you will get a very clear understanding of what kind of clarity you will need in your own life if you are going to succeed and live the best life possible. Remember, you get one life to live, so make sure you are going to live it well. Be clear about what you want, and watch your life flourish with greatness.

---

[1] http://www.merriam-webster.com/dictionary/clarity.

First, let's talk about what clarity is, in regards to what we want out of our lives or where we want to be in our lives. Unless you are clear about what you want, you might just end up with what you don't want. That alone should scare you. Can you imagine focusing time and energy and ending up with what you did not want? But it happens more often than we think. In fact, most people go through life with very little clarity of what they want out of life. In my case, I didn't change until I started to think for myself. In his book, *The Strangest Secret*, Earl Nightingale says that a person will do everything in the world to not have to think. In school we are taught what to think about, not how to think. For me, finding clarity was about taking the time to be intentional about what I wanted out of my life.

I once asked someone the question, "Did your job choose you or did you choose your job?" The woman thought about that for a moment and said, "I just needed a job at the time, and this was the job that was available." She has been with the same company for the last twenty-two years. Thankfully, she loves it. But many people aren't so lucky.

We sometimes never really find any clarity in our lives regarding what we want because we only take what's available to us. Millions of employees wake up each day and go to a job that they really don't like with a boss that they don't like. You could be living someone else's dream and not even realize it. But if that's the case, someone else could be living yours.

For many years I just lived with no real intention of doing anything great. But I had shown ambition at a young age, so I did have the potential. I just lost the drive somewhere along the way.

I was around seven or eight years old when I started my first business. I knew what I wanted to do, and that was to mow lawns. I was young, but this was the very first time I had some clarity on what I wanted to do for that season of my life. I went to my grandfather and asked him if I could use his lawn mower and of course he said yes, I could. Me and a couple of friends started to go around to houses, putting these horribly made homemade fliers on people's doors, advertising our business with my grandparents' phone number. When I got my very first *and only* job from the fliers, my grandfather drove me over to the house where we mowed someone's lawn for twenty bucks. It was exciting to get twenty dollars when I was that young, even though I had to split it with my friend who was my partner at that time, and of course my grandfather, who bought himself a beer with his share of the money.

Still, this was the first time I really knew I was capable of doing something that would actually matter. It planted this amazing seed of entrepreneurship that would grow one day into a giant tree. We all know that great trees take time to grow and can't be rushed if they are going to be great. And I sure did take my time.

As I said, working hard was not an issue for me—this was something I had programmed myself to do from when I was a child. However, using clarity would not really come into play until many years later when I began the planning stage of starting my very first official business. I knew I wanted to own my own business many years before I actually started one.

I was thirty-four years old, had a great job at the time working as a plumber, and had been in the field for about twelve years. One day I came home and told my wife that I wanted start a business in the plumbing industry. My wife was not totally surprised since I had mentioned it many times, and she was very supportive in this new endeavor. Since she had a degree in business, I knew she would be able to offer some insight, so I sought her advice.

I had absolute clarity with what I wanted the end result to be, but I wasn't sure about all the necessary steps. Still, by having the clarity I was able to evaluate exactly what it would take to make this happen. I also knew it would change my life forever.

Do You Live on Purpose?

By that I mean, do you live your life on purpose? Do you do the things you really want to do in this life? If having a job at a fast-food restaurant is what inspires you, if that is truly what you want out of life, then that is awesome. You are living on purpose. If you want to build a company from the ground up, that is also awesome.

Think about this for a moment: are you living on purpose to succeed, or living on purpose a life of failure and disappointment? From my own personal experience, most people I see are just living to fail and to stay miserable. Don't believe me? Just look around at your friends and family and the everyday people you see at work. Pay attention to those who are happy with where they are in life, and to those who are not happy with where they are in life. If you asked them if they are happy with where they are, the majority would tell you that they are *not happy* with where they are in their lives.

So the real question is: does this have to be this way? No, it does not! You have the ability today to start designing a brand-new life for yourself. You just have to stop and take some time to think about what you really want. This is where the clarity comes in; you have to know what it is you want before you can have what you want.

So, how does this work? How do I decide what it is that I want?

Remember this: Life is going to go by no matter what, and you have the choice to be where you are or where you want to be. The next ten years are going to go by and you have absolutely no control over that, but what you do have control over is what you are going to do over those next ten years. You will either be where you are, or where you want to be. Now you just have to decide where you want to be—and I mean define it down to the exact measure of what you want with such clarity that when you or anyone else looks at your goal they can say, without a doubt, that it is very clear.

Have you ever looked through a freshly cleaned glass window and said, “Wow! That is clear!” That is how you should be able to view what you want out of your life. You need to be able to look at what you want with that kind of clarity, because clarity, in my opinion, is the first step to creating any worthwhile goal. Remember, you can’t hit a target you can’t see. Imagine going to the shooting range and having no target to shoot at. It would be quite boring, not having anything to measure your progress against.

Examples of Clarity

Let's look at some examples of people who were very clear about what they wanted. Henry Ford had a desire to ease the life of farmers by creating some kind of vehicle to replace the farm animals having to do the work. He wanted to find a way to be more efficient with farming. Once he had created his first vehicle, he kept on with what his clear vision was, and that was to continue creating other vehicles to sell to the public.

When he invented the Model T car, it was selling so fast that he had to come up with an idea to make the process go quicker. Once again, he was clear about what he wanted, so he came up with the assembly line to build cars. He then set his sights on the impossible idea of the V8 engine. At least, this was impossible at first to the engineers working on it, saying it couldn't be done. But Henry Ford was persistent with what he wanted and would not take no for an answer.

At the time there were other V8 engines already out there, but they were put together in two and three parts being bolted together and typically those who had a V8 engine car were in the upper class. Henry Ford wanted to create a V8 engine that was affordable to the average consumer but in one piece, not in the typical two and three pieces like the others, so as to reduce the cost of the engine. His engineers thought this was impossible, but Henry Ford had a very clear vision of what he wanted and would not settle for anything less than that.

Now think about this for a minute—if he had not known what he wanted, he would have never been able to achieve what he achieved. This man started with a very clear vision of what he wanted and was able to get it by knowing what he wanted with absolute clarity. Now you may say he must have been a genius to be able to do all the things he set out to do. Well, that's a matter of opinion, if you ask me.

Henry Ford left school around the age of fifteen and went through an apprenticeship as a machinist. He did not have all the great formal education that so many people have, but what he did have was a very clear vision of what he wanted and he was willing to work hard to make that vision come true. He didn't use the excuse of a lack education or not having enough money or poor timing. Instead he started eating the elephant one bite at a time.

We shouldn't make excuses for why we can't get what we want out of our lives when so many others have started and succeeded with so much less than what we currently have. The way to avoid excuses is to have very clear set of goals and a burning desire deep within you that will push you beyond anything you could possibly imagine.

Think of an architect who is going to build an enormous building that will wow the world. He starts out with a very clear idea of what he wants this building to look like overall. Then he designs it down to the very last little detail. He makes notes about what each floor will look like, what kind of walls it will have, how thick they will be, and what kind of plumbing and electrical systems will be used—down to the smallest item. When you look at planning this way, and have a very clear idea of what you want, then this becomes a reality because you already know all the steps required.

Now imagine if you started building this massive amazing building but never decided what you wanted it to look like. You just woke up one day and said, "I am going to build the most amazing building anyone has ever seen!" You didn't think this through, get any advice from anyone, or even consider what you would need to do to just get this started. You just started building with no plan of action and no real vision of what you wanted your building to look like and as to what purpose it would serve. If you did this, you would waste so much money, time, and resources. And no one would really approach a building project this way—but we do it all the time with our lives. No wonder we don't get the results we expect.

Now don't use this as an excuse—just because you don't have *everything* all figured out, it doesn't mean you shouldn't start. I know from working in construction for many years, you have to have a plan and know what that plan is before you start, but you can start without a *full* plan in place. It is so much easier, and your odds of success will be greater, if you have an absolutely a clear vision of what you want. This is going to be what separates the good from the great. You can adjust your plan as you are building, but you need to have a plan.

So what is clarity? It is knowing, without any doubt, what you want to accomplish and by when you want to accomplish the thing you have set out to do. It is taking the time to define what you want and putting it down on paper so you can keep it before you each day as a constant reminder of where you are going. When you know what you want with clarity, you are more likely to get there than if you are just trying to always wing it. You can wing some things in life: A vacation can be a fun thing to wing at times. A date with your better half can be a lot of fun to wing now and then. But it is definitely not the way to go when it comes to the important things in life.

One of my favorite authors and speakers, Brian Tracy, will tell you that having clarity and a very clear vision of what you want is one of the first steps in creating success in your life. In fact, every great author I have read always goes back to knowing what you want. Imagine Donald Trump trying to build Trump Tower without having a clear plan of what he wanted. Do you for one minute think that he would even begin this massive task without first knowing what he wanted to do and knowing how to do it? If he did this without a detailed plan, it would be disastrous and could cause him to possibly lose everything he invested into the project. Why? Because if you embark on a great journey without knowing what you want your outcome to be, you will waste so much of your time and resources in learning what *not* to do.

Your life is no different. If you are just existing, with no real idea of what you want from this life, you wake up every day and go through the motions. I bet if you really took some time and wrote down your daily activities and then analyzed what you do, you would be amazed at how unfulfilling and maybe even boring your daily life is. That's harsh, yes. Hard to swallow, yes. But you only have this *one life to live* while you are here on earth, so why don't you make it the best life possible by starting to define what it is you really want? Don't waste another minute of your life; don't go through another day without at least trying to figure out what it is you want from yourself, and what you want to truly gain from this world. You are absolutely worth it!

You are not going to get it all figured out all at once. But you can certainly figure out the very next step to take to help you move forward.

Take a moment and think about this—What is the most important thing you would like to change about your life right now? You don't have to make a list of ten things; just think of one thing—whatever is nagging you right now, whatever you spend the most brainpower on. Would you like to be a better spouse? A better parent? Would you like to have a more fulfilling job? Would you like to finally attain a healthy lifestyle?

Decide on that one thing and build a plan around that. If need be, start building a plan around very *small goals* along the way to your ultimate goal. If it still seems like too big of a task, think of it this way: if you can plan a vacation, you can plan your life. So many people will spend hours and hours and even *days* and *weeks* planning a vacation, but they won't make much of an effort to plan a better life for themselves. Sure, you may say, that's because a vacation is fun! It's a break from the stress and monotony of daily life. And you'd be partially right. Vacations are meant to be fun. But so is your life! Nowhere in the daily life handbook does it say your everyday life has to be unfulfilling, or something to merely overcome and struggle through. If your plan for a better life includes a clear vision, attainable goals, and plenty of time for rest and play, you'll be amazed at how pleasant and fulfilling your days will become.

Make a List and Check It Twice

Once you have figured out what it is you want, write it down. And make sure you write down what you want in every part of your life—not in just one area. If you want to make a big change—in your relationships, your job, a new career path, weight loss—it will affect all areas of your life. As you plan for your new life, don't try to emulate someone else's life—make sure you are designing your *own* life. If you are trying to design a life that someone else is living, you will end up very disappointed.

Think about what you are passionate about. Think about what makes you smile, what motivates you. Start with what you feel like you can actually achieve first, because you will build upon this small success as you go. Imagine a snowball rolling down a hill—it keeps getting bigger and bigger as it rolls. This will be the same for you as you are figuring out what kind of life you really want for yourself. Don't become frustrated if you don't have all the answers, because they will come in time. Be patient with yourself and most important, be kind to yourself as you embark on this new journey. Praise yourself every chance you get and make that one thing a priority because you deserve it. As the great author Les Brown always says, "You have greatness within you." The more you do, and the more small successes you achieve, you will start to have that feeling of greatness.

Put It to Paper

I have provided an exercise with prompts for you to fill in to help guide the most common areas of your life—both for your personal and professional goals. Get busy designing your life like an architect would design an amazing building. When you start to write down your goals and the steps to achieve them, I want you to dream and dream big. Throw out all the self-limiting beliefs you have and as approach this with the mindset that you cannot fail.

Dorothea Brande, in her book *Wake Up and Live!*, says to "act as if you could not fail." Remember, you are either going to be living to fail in life, or living on purpose to succeed in life. Think like this as you write out what you want. Repeat this to yourself as you begin: "If I could not fail, no matter what, what would I want?" You are the architect of your life and you are designing your life the way you want it to be. Make this fun, exciting, and be creative!

I hope by now you are beginning to understand the importance of having clarity in your life. This is the first step to designing the most amazing life ever, and you have just taken the most important steps. Keep in mind, this will take work on your part. Now let's have fun and get busy!

Put It to Paper Exercise:

List your big goals and the smaller goals that will help you achieve them. For example, if a personal goal is to lose fifteen pounds, your smaller goals could be the following:

- Drink more water.
- Visit your doctor for your yearly checkup and to make sure that goal is on target.

- Cut back on snack foods and dessert for one week and measure the progress.
- Invest in some good athletic shoes for exercise.
- Walk for thirty minutes every day after dinner.

And remember, as you journal your goals, assume that you *cannot* fail. Throw out all of your self-limiting beliefs and be confident in your ability to keep moving forward.

Personal Goals

Big Goal:
Smaller Goals along the Way:

Big Goal:
Smaller Goals along the Way:

Big Goal:
Smaller Goals along the Way:

Professional Goals

Big Goal:

Smaller Goals along the Way:

Big Goal:

Smaller Goals along the Way:

Big Goal:

Smaller Goals along the Way:

Notes:

Notes

"One of the best uses of your time is to increase your competence in your key result areas."

~ Brian Tracy

Chapter 2

Competence

You've got to have it before you can reach your goal.

Now that you've taken the time to do the initial work in deciding what you want in some of the most important areas of your life, we will discuss the next steps, including adjusting your mindset.

In order to achieve success, you must become competent in whatever it is you have decided to do. After listening to an audio from Brendon Burchard, I learned there are four levels of competence:

- **The unconscious incompetent:** You don't even realize that you lack the necessary competence in order to reach your desired outcome in life.
- **The conscious incompetent**: You now realize that you lack the skills to reach your desired outcome. You are now conscious of the fact that you are not competent and you will need additional help to become the competent person you need to be in order to reach your desired outcome.

- **The conscious competent:** You are in the learning phase of developing competence and you are aware and conscious of everything going on in your world pertaining to your goals. You are developing the skills that will soon make you an unconscious competent person.
- **The unconscious competent**: This is where you now have the competence needed to accomplish your desired outcome and you no longer think about it, as this now is ingrained into your DNA.

A great example of this is when you start learning to drive for the first time. The first time you get behind the wheel, you are what I call a conscious competent, as you are aware of everything going on around you. You see and think about every little move you make, every little change in direction, or every move others make around you while you are driving. You don't know all the rules so someone else (hopefully) is teaching you what you need to know.

The more you do this and the more competent of a driver you become, you eventually find yourself no longer thinking about driving and everything going on around you, but you automatically do this without even thinking about it. This is what I call being unconsciously competent. You are still aware, but you are aware in an unconscious manner because driving has become second nature.

Now that we know what the different levels of competence are, and once you have decided on an outcome or goal for your life, you can become a competent person in order to reach your desired outcome.

In the first chapter I shared some of my own personal stories of being in business, about having to find clarity in doing what I wanted to do. Once I had clarity, I still had a problem when I decided to start—I did not know enough about the business side of what I wanted to do, so I lacked a major part of becoming a successful entrepreneur. I lacked the knowledge and education of starting a business, and also the competency of being a business owner.

For me, the first step was becoming self-employed. Being self-employed and being a business owner are two very different things. Being self-employed means that the business depends solely on you as the owner to make the revenue for the business; being an actual business owner means your business runs off systems where the business does not solely depend on you to be there in order for it to function. I had to become a competent person if I was to be successful in my start of my first business.

So what did I do? I quit a very nice paying job with no real future, as far as growth potential. Leaving my place of employment would be taking away the only certainty that I knew. Remember I had been laid off fourteen times before, so intentionally giving up job security was a bit of a challenge for me. Since I had struggled financially for so many years of my life, having a great job was a blessing to me. But I *knew* I wanted more.

Once I'd decided on my plan of action, I spent the next six months preparing myself to start my own plumbing company before I quit my current job. I purchased books on how to start a plumbing business from two different generations of master plumbers; they discussed everything from marketing, finance, loans, customer service, and anything you would find yourself doing in a business. I studied everything there was about starting and launching my first business as a self-employed individual, but you will can so much from reading a book. At some point, I knew would have to act on this new knowledge.

It Takes Courage

During this same six-month period, as I was studying, I was also developing the courage to actually make this happen. I remember the day I walked into the shop I was working for and told them I was quitting and starting a business. When I sat down at the lunch table and said I was giving my resignation, they looked a little shocked—and I understood. I had been there for eight years. I loved the job I had with them; they treated me like a king. It was a truly great job.

When I said why I was resigning, one of the owners said, "So you're going to be my competition, are you?" He instantly felt threatened, but he had nothing to worry about. The company I worked for was a large company that did mostly large commercial jobs. The business I was getting into was the residential service side of the business. Same skills, different market. Still, the mood changed to a very somber and uncomfortable feeling. I could see the disappointment in my boss's eyes. But I knew I would never go any further than where I was as an employee. I wanted more out of life, and I was willing to do whatever it took to get myself there. In the end, they respected my two-weeks' notice and allowed me to continue my work there.

Prepare for the Day

Remember, I had spent the last six months secretly preparing myself for the day I would walk out of that shop with a new adventure in hand. I had already purchased my first van, tools to go in the van, the financial software I would use, and software for my company's price book so I'd know what I would charge my customers. I had created a workable marketing plan and my wife and I created our first website. So even though it was tough to give my notice and walk away, I was ready when I quit my job. And I did it respectfully, because you don't burn the bridge that supports you until you have built a different bridge.

So let's talk about what *you* want now. If you took the time at the end of the last chapter to write down your goals, you are one step closer to greatness. If you did not take the time to write those down, you are now still one step behind. Doing the work necessary to achieve greatness can be one of the biggest but most rewarding challenges you are ever faced with.

My advice is to not start any business until you know everything you can about it and feel comfortable doing so. (Notice how I said, "everything you can"? You'll likely never know everything you possibly can about a business or market. But you can do the work to find out everything that is available to be known by you at your current stage in the process.) You may never feel comfortable starting and launching a new endeavor, but don't let that become your excuse to not start. Starting is one of the hardest things sometimes you will ever do. Just take some time to understand what you are about to do to increase your odds of success.

Before we take the next step, let's look at an example. Let's say you set some goals for your marriage. You have now stated the goal of having a better marriage, and you've written down your list of clear goals and know exactly what you want it to look like. You have the idea of what you want, but now you need to educate yourself on what you have to do to reach your marital goals. Can you believe you might actually have to learn some things about marriage in order to have an amazing marriage? This might mean you will have to read some specific books on marriage, or maybe go to some really good marriage seminars to learn how to develop some new skills to get what you want out of your marriage. When it comes to you feeling competent while working toward your desired outcome, it is inevitably going to take some training to get what you want.

When we have not been trained in what we want, we tend to make so many more mistakes than we really care to share. Especially when it comes to marriage—it took me three times to get it right! I had no idea as to what a good marriage looked like, and no idea how to even make or participate in a good marriage. It took me learning the hard way, but I did.

Take the time to learn from others' successes and mistakes so you can make your life the best ever—and avoid being a negative statistic. Almost 50 percent of all marriages end up in divorce; 50 percent of all new businesses fail in the first five years, and 90 percent within ten years. If we just took a little more time to become competent in what we are doing, I personally believe our lives would be so different—and better—in most areas of our lives.

Because I took the time and prepared for my business, it was so much easier for me to start my new venture; it also relieved so much of the stress I knew I could possibly face. No, it wasn't easy to walk away from the security of the weekly paycheck I had grown so accustomed to. I started a new business without *any* customers and just a goal of being my own boss and living the American dream. But I did have a great support system with my wife and my kids. As of today, I have been in business for over six years and I have to tell you that it has been an ever-evolving positive experience.

Becoming competent never stops; it just evolves into other areas of your business or life. Things will always change, so make sure you are always looking at ways to stay competent—whether that's attending training sessions, networking events, seminars, reading or listening to audio books, or working with mentors. We need to make sure we are always learning everything we can. One of my favorite acronyms is "CAN I?" This stands for "Constantly Always Needing Improvement." The answer—always—is yes! You can!

So many people never take the time to become competent when it comes to starting a new project or a new business, so they seem to fail very quickly and just give up. You can't take shortcuts either, as this will only get you so far, and then all of a sudden you are knocked out of the game with one simple blow. You have to take the time to prepare yourself to succeed, or more than likely, you will be left where you started.

A total lack of competence is another giant killer of most projects we start. A person who is always starting something and never really finishes it usually doesn't know enough about what he or she is doing, so frustrated comes quickly. Then he or she moves on to the next exciting thing until burning out there as well. You can have fifteen unfinished projects or fifteen unmet goals—or one finished project or goal achieved. Which scenario do you prefer?

I once heard Donald Trump say that the reason he is so successful in starting new things is that he takes so much time in preparing for what he is about to do before he does it. This is simple logic of becoming a competent person in reaching your goals and desired outcome. At least, you *think* it would be simple logic. So take the time and prepare yourself to be a competent person in the areas in which you want to improve. This might mean you will have to go to college, go to some continuing education classes, or it could be just as simple as reading a book.

You may say, "I don't have the money," or "I don't have the resources," or "I don't know who to talk to about what I need to learn." Those are just excuses and nothing more. Ever heard of Google? Start with your public library—this place is full of so many great resources on becoming competent on anything you want in your life. And the best part about this is it only takes a library card. I have personally spent *thousands* of dollars on books, audio programs, and DVDs to learn to be the person I wanted to be. You don't have to pay a lot of money for the information you need when there are other ways to get the same information for just the cost of a library card or an Internet search.

Seek Out Experts

Popular author and speaker Anthony Robbins often talks about how he would go to the book store to buy everything he could about the subjects he wanted to learn about. When he didn't have enough money, he would have to come back over and over again until he was able to get all the things he wanted. He used whatever resources he had to accomplish his end result. And he never allowed there to be an excuse as to why he couldn't do it. Instead, he found every excuse as to why he *could* do it.

Another of my favorite authors, Brian Tracy, found that when he was in his early twenties, based on the level of education he had, his life was going nowhere. He hadn't graduated from high school, and was taking different labor jobs that were all dead ends. Finally he came to the realization that if he wanted to have a better life, he needed to make changes. Brian decided what he wanted to do and then took the steps to become competent in his life. He went to college, got a master's degree in business, has now written over fifty books, and is one of the most sought-after speakers out there.

Neither of these men would have ever reached their level of success if they had not taken the time to become a more competent person in regards to what they wanted. Just like them, you are going to have to do the legwork to get what you want. You can't expect someone else to do it for you. Both Brian Tracy and Anthony Robbins chose to make sure they knew everything they could about the fields they were getting into. I know I could not have ever reached the success I have if I had not made learning a majority priority in my life. Remember, I wasn't one who liked going to school or learning when I was younger. At some point I realized that if I did not do something to change my circumstances, I might be delivering pizzas the rest of my life.

I have spent the last fifteen years constantly learning and growing. In fact, I have made growth and knowledge some of my greatest priorities. I've spent my driving hours listening to CDs about business, personal development, success, relationships, and coaching. I spend time every day learning something new about where I want to be in my life. This will have to become a priority in your life, too, if you are going to move forward in reaching your goals.

Remember the question, how does one eat an elephant? The answer is simple—one bite at a time. When it comes to you working toward becoming a competent person in reaching your goals, do it one day at a time. One item at a time. Don't stress over how long it might take you. Time is going to go by, no matter what you do, so you might as well spend the time working toward a worthwhile goal. I don't want to get to the end of my life and wish I had done something about what I wanted. No matter how old you are, you can still start. You get to create your new beginning and your new ending.

Your Thoughts Will Lead You

Another author, Earl Nightingale, shares a story in his famous audio called *The Strangest Secret* about trying to understand why some people are successful and others are not. He went on a journey, searching for the answer, and spent many years trying to understand this phenomena. He found a little book in the library (see, I said library) called *Think and Grow Rich* by Napoleon Hill. In this book, he found what he called the "secret to success," and that is to think. He found if you could just *think* about what you wanted, you could get where you wanted to go.

Most people will never to really take the time to think about what they want. Every great idea always starts with a thought. So stop making excuses and start working on becoming a competent person in order to achieve what you want out of life. Tell yourself—right now—you can reach your goal. Decide right now what it is you are going to have to do and what you are going to have to learn to become a competent person. This is the key to your success.

Then take some time and look at the goals you have set for yourself. Ask yourself the question, "What do I have to learn, and who do I have to become in order to reach the goals I have set for myself? What am I willing to do to make sure my life turns out the way I want?" You can't live your life jealous of others when you have the very same ability to do more than you have already done.

Remember to keep this process fun, as this will help you to learn more quickly. When you are in a relaxed state of mind, you will learn things much more quickly. If you can find a friend to help you with your goals, it can be more enjoyable and you will find that two minds can be so much more creative than one. Share some of your ideas with your family and friends. Dream your dream and live your dream.

Make *your* life a priority. You can do this!

Notes:

"Without a humble but reasonable confidence in your own powers you cannot be successful or happy." *~ Norman Vincent Peale*

Chapter 3
Confidence

When you have it, you're going to fly.

According to the Merriam Webster online dictionary, *confidence* is "a feeling or belief that you can do something well or succeed at something," or that you have the "a feeling of belief that someone or something is good or has the ability to succeed at something."[2] Now that you know what it is you want to do with your life, and you have decided to do the things necessary to become a competent person in order to reach your desired goals, you now need to understand the value of confidence. Your confidence level will determine how far you go in life.

Having never graduated high school, nor attended college, I used to look down on myself because of my lack of education. I made up so many excuses as to why I could not do the things I dreamed of doing in my life. I lacked confidence in myself because I was spending so much time comparing myself to other people. This is a huge killer in so many lives, as we are always judging ourselves based on what others have done. I have always believed

---

[2] http://www.merriam-webster.com/dictionary/confidence.

that I could *accomplish* anything, but I still found time to procrastinate and make excuses.

I missed out on so many opportunities because I lacked confidence. I even remember being scared to talk to people, even though I knew it could have an amazing impact on my life. I ran from opportunity because I was not confident in talking to people who were more educated than myself. Because I judged myself and gave myself the label of "uneducated," I automatically saw others as being better than me.

Because I have struggled with confidence in the past, I now easily recognize a lack of confidence in others, including an individual I once coached. This guy was personal trainer in the fitness industry and wanted to grow his business. He knew what he wanted to do and recognized what he needed to know in order to become a competent person and in order to run a successful personal training business. On a scale of 1 to 10, he gave himself a 5 in regards to fitness training. So I gave him some simple homework to get him to a higher level of competence that would automatically raise his confidence levels, because competence automatically raises your confidence. But just because you are competent in what you are doing, it does not mean you will have the *immediate* confidence to do what is necessary to reach your goals.

It was very apparent that he lacked the confidence to walk up to a total stranger to talk about his business. I know so many people would rather die first than want to talk to a total stranger, but when you are in the fitness business, you have to be willing to talk to people—even total strangers—because they're all potential clients! You'll have to overcome the fear, step out of your comfort zone, and do it anyway, or you will limit yourself and your potential growth. Sadly, he wasn't able to overcome his fear of talking to strangers. This also ended up being the one and only coaching session I had with him. He never reached out again to try and become better at what he was doing. I later watched this same individual leave the fitness industry to get a "normal" job. He could have had all the knowledge he needed, but he allowed his fear to overwhelm his dream. Just like him, your lack of confidence in what you are doing can be the death of your career if you don't overcome it.

Now, I sympathized with this man. I completely understood how he felt about fear. I struggled with it when I wanted to start my own company, and I struggled with it again when I wanted to become a life and success coach. Without even realizing it, I kept comparing myself to others and the education that they had. Then one day I had an epiphany and realized I had been coaching people for *years* without realizing it. I have devoted thousands of hours learning about business development, personal development, marriage development, relationship development, leadership development, and so on. But since my education did not come from a college class, I saw myself as less valuable than those coaches who went to college. Still, I repeatedly saw people change their thinking and their lives based on our conversations. I was already a *coach.* I knew the value I could give to others. I just lacked the confidence to sell my services as one.

My studies came from reading books, attending seminars, and hiring mentors who were the very best in the industry. These people had already achieved what I wanted to achieve in my own life. When I began to really compare apples to apples, I came to the conclusion that I have had some of the *best education* in the world. I stopped comparing myself to other people and stopped making excuses. I've now been a life and success coach for several years and I absolutely love it.

To be honest, you will have to get *some kind* of education no matter what you do. But it doesn't always have to come with a *degree*. If you should choose college to be your source of education, then I can assure you that you will have an amazing group of educators who can get you where you want to be in life. If you should choose to self-educate, then I suggest you find the very best in the industry you want to serve, read every book, and listen to every audio they offer to make sure you are getting the best self-education you can possibly get.

When I started my first business, I had to have confidence in who I was and in my skill set. In order to gain a customer, I had to show confidence so the customer would believe in me. If a customer saw my confidence, they automatically assumed I was competent! I don't care how *competent* you are, if you aren't confident in what you are doing, the customer will see right through you and not want to do any business with you. Whether right or wrong, people equate a lack of confidence with a lack of competence.

Case in point: I have a friend who is a *master* at what he does, but he has no confidence in himself and it continues to hurt his career. I have watched him struggle for years. No matter how much encouragement or advice I share with him, if *he doesn't believe he's worth it*, he won't adopt a new mindset or new behaviors to support his growth. This is so frustrating to me, because he is one of the nicest guys I have ever met. But if a person can't find a way to believe in his or her own abilities, failure is inevitable.

I once sat down and asked a sixty-five-year-old man what his greatest regrets were in his life. His number-one regret was that he did not try harder in his first marriage. He was married for eighteen years, and never really made the effort to make his marriage a good marriage. Decades later he still regrets not trying harder. Unfortunately, this happens to many people in so many areas of our lives. If we never take the time to understand how to be good at what we want to do, when we get older we will look back on our lives with regret.

If You Build It, They Will Come

Building confidence is a lot like building muscles. If you've ever worked on your fitness, you know that it takes effort and consistency in order to enlarge your muscles. So let's consider how a muscle grows. In order to build muscle, you'd start out with the five- or ten-pound weights for the first two weeks, and then the next week add another five pounds until eventually you are using the fifty-pound weights and your muscles have grown in size and strength. Not only will this new physique show physically; it will also show in your attitude and personality. You put in hours of hard work, and you're pleased with the results, confident in your ability to become healthier and fit. Your self-image has just sky rocketed!

Do you see how this is the same technique to follow for any goal you want to achieve? When you start building confidence, you start with a couple of small things you know you can do and continue building on them. Just like you wouldn't walk into the gym on your first day and try to bench press three hundred pounds (at least, I hope not), you wouldn't want to overcome your fear of public speaking by getting on stage for the very first time in front of two thousand people and having it televised! You'd take baby steps, slowly building confidence at each stage along the way until one day you were ready and excited about stepping on stage in front of a large audience.

When you're starting to work on your confidence, a good tip is to write down every successful thing you have ever done, no matter how small it was. And yes, I do mean everything you can possibly think of. It could have been getting a ribbon for a fourth-grade spelling bee, getting an "A" on a difficult school paper, or it could have been winning a bowling tournament. No matter what your experiences, write down as many of these "wins" as you can remember, even if it takes you thirty minutes and five sheets of paper. The more lines you can fill, the more you should appreciate all of the great things you've already accomplished, which can be a great way to boost your confidence in tackling this new goal.

The more you practice doing what you are afraid of, the easier it will get. A good example of someone who might suffer from lack confidence is a salesman. So many people are scared of the word *no*. Can you imagine that the word *no* could actually scare someone? But it happens every day—two little letters scaring the life out of you. I know about this from the first-hand experience of owning a business and having employees who were scared to death of the word *no*. They were so scared of rejection that they would do everything they could to avoid the closing part of the sale, or they'd sell the product for a smaller amount of money, or not make any effort to sell the product to the customer at all.

The only way to get over this fear is to just do the thing that scares you. This kind of fear is not a logical fear; it is a made up one in our minds. There's no *real* danger here. Dale Carnegie, in his book *How to Stop Worrying and Start Living*, says to ask yourself what's the worst that can happen, and when you have come up with the worst-case scenario, ask yourself if you can live with the results. If you can live with the results, then that takes away the fear.

Fear stands for "False Evidence Appearing Real." Tell yourself that you can do "it" everyday—whatever "it" is for you—and you will start believing you can and your life will change. You can also get a little creative and instead of avoiding your fear, start rewarding your efforts in overcoming it! I once heard a story of a sales trainer who created a contest for all the sales people to see who could get the most no's in the day. When the employees realized the only way to hear a "no" or to win the contest was to take action, they became more and more comfortable when they heard the word *no*. They worked hard each day trying to talk to as many customers as possible to win this prize and they came to the realization that the word *no* is nothing more than a word. This took the pressure off of them to perform, but in the end it also developed the skill to get and close more sales, as they were calling and talking to more prospects.

The more you go out of your way to do that one thing that is holding you back, the quicker you will be able to build your confidence to a level so high that nothing can stop you. Your self-image will jump to heights you never imagined once you start facing the fears that are holding you back. Once your self-image jumps to new heights, everyone around you will see you as a different person. This is going to be what helps catapult you to the life you have always dreamed of having.

Breaking Down to Build Back Up

Let's look at how the U.S. military creates confidence. Two of my sons have gone into the military—one in the United States Air Force and one in the United States Army. Both branches use the same techniques to build the soldier up—they start by breaking you down and teaching you the very basics. They would never just throw you into a special forces training when you just get in—that would be absurd. Instead they start you on a training regimen that is doable for the average beginning soldier. They first have to build you up by doing repetitive things every day, which builds your competence level for the job ahead.

When my son went into the Air Force for basic training he weighed around 218 pounds, but when he got out of basic training he weighed less than 200 pounds, was able to run for miles at a time, and do things physically that he was not able to do before he entered basic training. The U.S. military specializes in creating lasting confidence in their troops. So you go through boot camp, which is the phase that will prepare you to be a tried and true soldier. If you do not have what it takes to make it through boot camp, then more than likely you will not be allowed to stay in the military. If you do make it through boot camp and decide that you want to go into the Special Forces, you will be challenged again. But making through boot camp is a confidence-building experience, and you are probably excited and ready for the new training challenges. You have spent the last couple of months preparing to be a true warrior, and you are physically fit enough to start the new adventure. Your confidence has been boosted from the first day you started your training by doing things each day with a very specific purpose, which was to build your competency and confidence as a soldier.

It's the same with any goal you want to accomplish. The more you do it over and over, the more your confidence builds. Give yourself a routine that you can follow each day with a very specific purpose. Design your day with that purpose in mind, knowing it is going to give you the outcome you have set out to create. Do this on a daily basis so you create a habit and become the very best you.

I have heard it said many times that if you will just do the thing you fear, then that fear is sure to disappear. So ask yourself right now, "What can I specifically do right now to help me gain the confidence I need to reach the goals I have set for myself?" Take time to really consider this; if you're unsure, ask your colleagues or friends. Find someone who has succeeded in what you are trying to do and ask him or her what he or she did to become so successful. Allow their explanation and story to build *your* confidence that the goal can indeed be achieved.

A great scripture in the Bible, Proverbs 15:22 says there is wisdom in the midst of counsel. If you don't know anyone who can give advice or you are to scared to ask for help, by all means go to the library or book store and get yourself a minimum of three books on the subject and put what you learn into practice. You can even ask the librarian or the customer service rep in the bookstore for some good books on the specific subject. They might have or know exactly what it is you need. If you still need a little boost of confidence, go look in the mirror and make sure you let yourself know how valuable you are and that you have what it takes to do this. And if you are still scared to do the necessary things that will ultimately build your confidence, find a friend who will help you get out of your comfort zone. If you're an adrenaline junkie and you need to slap fear in the face, you could even jump out of an airplane to boost your confidence!

Author and speaker Anthony Robbins conducts an event called "Unleash the Power Within." On the first night of the event, he does an exercise that is sure to help you overcome any fear you might have. Believing that fear is just a mental block that you have developed over the years of your life, Robbins has participants do a fire walk. *Yes, a real fire walk.* He has all of the participants walk across burning coals as way to overcome their negative beliefs and fear they've been holding on to for years.

Now, in my opinion, this sounded pretty scary—until I heard about the preparation that happens *before* the fire walking. One of my coaching clients shared that she attended one of these "Unleash the Power Within" events. Robbins spent the first part of the evening mentally preparing the audience for what they were about to do. Some would say that this is like psyching yourself out to get the job done. When it was her turn, she was a little scared but they would not let her go until they *knew* she was ready to make that walk. When she walked across the hot coals, she kept her focus on the individuals on the other side, coaching her across. She made it across unhurt but invigorated in so many ways. It was important for her to stay focused on her outcome while she was walking, in order for her not to become scared of the fire under her feet. Her self-confidence skyrocketed! She had accomplished something she never imagined she could do. The best part for her was that she crushed her fear and lack of confidence; she knew if she could do this, she could conquer the world.

After that event she went home, took a good look at her life, and decided she wanted a change. She quit her job and opened her own business because she now had the confidence to do it. She always *knew* what she wanted to do, she was already very competent in her line of work, but she lacked the one thing that would propel her to where she wanted to be—confidence.

Sometimes you may have to do something as crazy as walking on fire. Maybe you just need to join a Toastmasters club to overcome your fear of public speaking. If you can overcome any fear, then you can overcome what is holding you back. You have to make developing self-confidence an absolute priority in your life. If you don't start building this muscle of confidence, then you will not move forward. You may end up staying exactly where you are. In the normal course of life, you are going to be challenged in so many ways that you cannot even imagine, and you are going to need this muscle of confidence to be as big as possible. But if jumping out of a plane or walking across fire isn't for you, there's always the trapeze!

Author and speaker Allison Maslan uses the trapeze—flying high in the sky from one side of the set to the other—as a way to help her clients overcome their fears and show them how to build self-confidence within themselves. Maslan has a passion for the trapeze, and she has used this to help her muscle of confidence stay strong. Whatever means you find, you need to find *something* that can help you create the confidence you need to succeed in life. There are so many ways you can develop your confidence and soar to new heights of living if you will just try. You never have to stay where you are.

Decide today that you are going to purposefully do whatever it takes to build that muscle of confidence. Make this a priority in your life. Start today with even the smallest thing that scares you—and just do it. You have what it takes within you to overcome any fear you could imagine, if you would just trust the power God has put within you to do great things. Trust yourself and know that you have exactly what it takes to be great.

Notes:

Notes

"You need to make a commitment and once you make it, then life will give you some answers."

~ Les Brown

Chapter 4
Commitment

With this, you will go far.

Let's review what we have learned so far. We discussed clarity, which means we are very clear (or we are getting very clear) on what we want for our lives. Then we learned about competence, knowing we are going to do whatever it takes to become a competent person for the desired outcome. We also talked about confidence and how we have to do some exercises to develop the muscles of our confidence.

Now it's time to start a conversation about having a commitment to getting what we want. We can have everything else figured out, but if we don't have commitment, then we might as well not even waste our time working on the rest. This is going to be one of the most important deciding factors that determines if you ever get what you want out of life.

Take the guys or gals who want to get in good physical shape in order to look and feel great. Maybe they are currently overweight and have been struggling with losing the weight but cannot seem to make time to commit to becoming who they want to become. They continue to look in the mirror at someone they don't like, but there is not enough pain associated in what they see to push them to commit to eating right, exercising more, and doing the things necessary to get where they want to be.

Your commitment to your goals will be necessary for your success in anything you do. It starts with a decision to be committed to your goal, and then it goes to building the daily and weekly habits to keep you going. It seems to always start out as a challenge when you start working toward something new. This is the most normal thing you will ever encounter. When you start working out with weights and you haven't done it in many years, you might be excited at first until the next day when you feel the physical pain of working out. This is going to be the same in pursuing anything in life. You will unconsciously look for any excuse to quit if you have not built up the habits of completing the things you start, no matter the discomfort.

I'll share a secret with you: it takes as much time to quit something as it does to keep going because time is just that—it is time. Time is no respecter of persons. Time doesn't care if you are rich or poor, strong or weak, big or small. Time is going to go by no matter what, and the difference between those who will be successful in life and those who won't is the fact that some stick to what they have started and some don't. Most give up and never push themselves to a place where they feel ecstatic about what they have created in their lives.

Those who decide to climb Mount Everest first start out by expressing interest that this is something they want to do. They research what is required and they start the physical training for the massive climb they are about to embark on. They go to what they call a lower base camp to start getting acclimated to the lower oxygen levels they will encounter. During this time, many will drop out, as they will see that this journey may now seem a little too much for them. Once they start to feel what oxygen deprivation feels like, it can be uncomfortable for them and also a little scary. If they see others fail all around them to reach the summit, as they climb, they'll think of the stories of those who lay lifeless on the path ahead—and many who still lay frozen in death on the path to the summit. But if they keep their eyes ahead and their focus strong, they can achieve the climb.

There are many issues that can be a great deterrent in accomplishing the goals you have set for yourself. You are going to be faced with so many obstacles on the way to your destination, but if you can build the habit of committing yourself to completing small goals, then when you get to the bigger goals, they will not seem big at all because you are used to finishing what you start.

Staying committed to my goals has been challenging at many times, especially when the road seemed to fall out from under me. But when the road falls out from under you, go and build a new bridge over the road. Find a way no matter how hard it seems.

Commitment is one of those things most people are not willing to do when it comes to a major goal or desired outcome. Just the thought of commitment can scare people away from working toward any worthwhile goal. Marriage is certainly one of the goals that takes a lot of commitment. Many people in a relationship run from the very thought of marriage because of the enormous commitment this will take. Think of all the people you know who have run from a commitment—no matter the goal. Now evaluate your own life. What kinds of goals have you put off because of a fear of commitment? Write down some of the things you wanted to do that you decided *not to do* because you were scared of committing and following through.

Once, while on a family vacation in Maui, Hawaii, with our girls, we were at a place called Black Rock in Kaanapali Beach. We swam out to jump off the cliffs, along with all the others doing it. Of our three girls, two of them are daring and brave and the other . . . well, let's just say she doesn't like crazy adventures much. I took my then-eleven-year-old daughter (the courageous one of the bunch) to the top with me. When we got to the top, we realized immediately that the jump seemed much higher from the top looking down than it did from the water looking up. So I told her, “Listen, I want you to make absolutely sure you want to do this, because when we jump there is no turning back.” Imagine telling your eleven-year-old daughter there is no turning back, and what that might make her feel like inside. She said she wanted to jump so I grabbed her hand and said let’s go—and we jumped! She was so glad she did it, and so excited that she committed to the jump.

Sometimes when you make a commitment to something, you have to be committed to not turning back. Other times, I think the problem is that people are scared to commit to something because they are scared of the amount of time it might take to accomplish what they want to do. You will never have anything great if you are not willing to commit to whatever it is you are setting out to do. This might take some serious patience. When students decide that the profession they are going to pursue is to become a doctor, they have to realize the commitment it is going to take in order to become a doctor. The average time it takes to become a doctor is around twelve years. That’s a long time, isn’t it? A doctor has to finish the typical four years of college and then the four years of medical school and then another three to six years of residency work. This doesn't include additional time if you are specializing in something. Becoming a doctor takes some serious commitment. It also means you will have to have a lot of patience.

When I was a single parent with three boys to raise, I was making just under nine dollars an hour. This was really tough on a recently divorced parent. At the time, it was really tough to stay committed to a job that showed such little reward. I needed money *now* and I did not want to wait the five years it was going to take to be making a good income as a plumber. I was in an apprenticeship at the time, and I had an opportunity to take another job making a couple of dollars more an hour, which would have helped me for the time being, but meant that I would lose the long-term opportunity I had coming to me if I stayed committed to the goal of completing that apprenticeship. So I talked to my boss and explained my situation to him, telling him I wasn't making enough, and it was forcing me to have to look for another job. Right there, on the spot, I got a nice raise, greater than what I would have had if I had left and went to that other company. I stayed committed to that apprenticeship so by the end of it, I was making around thirty-two dollars an hour. I just had to keep my focus on my goal and where I *would* be.

So many of us lose our focus on where we want to be and we trade out the ultimate goal for a cheaper version because we aren't willing to stay committed to the long-term process of reaching the original coveted goal. The one thing about commitment is you need to count the cost of *what you are about to do* to make sure you are going to be committed to doing what you want to do. Did you get that? You need to count the cost first—of both quitting what you are doing to start something new, and of staying in the same place—so you don't fall into the trap of constantly starting things and not finishing them.

How many unfinished books do you think are out there? I'm sure there are thousands upon thousands of unfinished manuscripts that no one will ever read. Anthony Robbins says you have to turn your *shoulds* into *musts*. When you turn your commitment into an absolute must, there will be nothing that will hold you back. When Jack Canfield wrote the book *Chicken Soup for the Soul*, he was turned down by over a 144 publishers before he found someone to publish his book. That took some serious commitment! I can guarantee most people would have given up after just a couple of times being told no. His absolute commitment to getting his book published turned out to be a pretty amazing thing, as he has sold millions and millions of his books. When you are committed to what you want, great things will happen and great opportunities will come before you if you will just stay committed.

Think of Thomas Edison—the process of creating the light bulb took some serious commitment. Imagine doing something *ten thousand times* before you finally succeeded. Think about this for a second: it has been said that Edison *failed* in creating the light bulb almost 10,000 times before he succeeded! That took a a *serious* commitment.

Are you that committed to reaching your goals? Do your goals matter that much to you? What is the driving factor that will keep you motivated? The best thing you can do when something doesn't go right is to stop and analyze why it didn't go right. Ask yourself what could you have done differently. What will you do next? Whatever you're working on or toward, you are going to need to have a big enough reward at the end of the tunnel in order to keep you going. Daily affirmations of telling yourself you are committed to reaching your goals are going to be an amazing source of encouragement to you in this process. Most important, having a physical and mental picture of the end result will keep you going.

Are your goals big enough with a big enough reward at the end to keep you committed to doing whatever it will take to accomplish them? At the end of the day, you can either pay the price for what you want, or pay the price of living somebody else's life. You may need to employ a team or group to help you stay committed to the ultimate success you desire. Don't employ Negative Nancy or Debbie Downer to be on your team of motivators. Rather make sure you have a group of optimists who are smarter and more positive than you are.

Each time I wanted to give up, I had to really change what I was focusing on so I could see all the possible solutions rather than the problems at hand. Commitment takes focus like you have never imagined. To that end, here's a couple of very important things you can do today to make sure you stay committed when you start a project:

1. Create a vision board of exactly what you want from life. This is going to be a picture of what the end result looks like in your mind.

2. Get an accountability partner who understands what you want to do and who will help you stay the course. Make sure you find someone who is not a pessimist, but rather an optimist who is going to keep you positive and motivated.

3. Keep a journal that lets you know how you have done each day. You cannot measure what you do not track. It is so much easier to stay motivated when you know how you are doing.

Let's stay focused on where you want to go and make this life of yours the dream you want it to be!

Notes:

"Courage is being scared to death and saddling up anyway." ~ *John Wayne*

Chapter 5

Courage

When you find it, the world will know.

It's time to talk about courage. This one is the most amazing traits you can develop in your life, and it can also be one of the toughest ones to develop. It will be the little things you do every day that will make all the difference.

If you could travel back in time and look at the activities that required tremendous courage, or what you thought took tremendous courage, what would you see? Would you see true courage or would you see dumb luck? Sometimes we mistake our actions as courage, especially when we're younger. I made plenty poor choices as a kid and called it courage. So when I was more mature, I had to reevaluate my own definition of courage.

When I was seven years old, I used to steal my grandfather's cigarettes, climb a tree, and smoke them in secret. I didn't know you were supposed to inhale the smoke (thankfully). I just puffed on the cigarette and blew the smoke out because I'd watched my grandfather do for many years. I wanted to look cool, especially to my friends. This is a little crazy when you think about wanting to look cool at such a young age. But this should also show you that anything we do in front of younger kids sets an example for them to want to follow.

I thought it took courage to sneak into his drawer to get them because if I got caught for doing something wrong, I got the switch, and I knew that the pain was going to be hard to bear! My grandfather never said anything to me, so I never knew if he realized someone was stealing cigarettes. I got away with "courage" *that time*.

One day a friend and I were flying paper airplanes, and one of them flew up on the roof of the house—our two-story house. How were we going to get it down? I had my friend go out on the roof to get the paper airplane. My grandfather heard a noise, walked out of the house, and asked me if anyone was on the roof. I lied to his face—I said no one was on the roof. At that moment, a paper airplane flew off of the roof and my grandfather looked up and saw my friend standing there. He took that switch and whipped my butt all the way up the stairs! I thought my stupidity really was courage, and unfortunately I didn't grow out of that mindset until well into my adult years.

At sixteen, my friends and I would drive the country back roads in the area. Just for fun, someone would get on the top of the car and hold on from both sides, with their arms wrapped all the way across the top of the car, and the car would speed down the old dirt roads, the guy on top holding on for dear life, until the car stopped. It all ended when one of the guys fell off the car, and the driver threw the car into reverse and hit the guy on the ground, breaking his ribs. Then he took off and left us out there in the middle of the road with no ride home. It was a miracle my friend survived with only a few broken ribs! We got lucky when another of our friends just happened to drive past and he was able to give us a ride back.

I thought I was courageous when I would ride my bicycle down the road past mean dogs who were pretty darn fast but somehow never caught me. I thought I was courageous when I hid behind some bushes and shot my neighbor in the behind with a slingshot while he was out taking the trash. These weren't the smartest things to do, but believe it or not, this kind of stupidity was preparing me to be truly courageous when I got older because I was very familiar with taking chances.

Once, when my wife and I were on vacation with our kids, we went to a carnival where a slingshot ride would launch two people at a time into the air. As many crazy stunts I pulled as a kid, I was a chicken and had no courage to do this. My two girls who were eight and twelve years old sure didn't have any problem doing it. When I watched that thing launch them into the air, it made my stomach drop. On another occasion, while vacationing in Hawaii on the island of Maui, we went parasailing eight hundred feet into the air. I was apprehensive when we took off out into the water, hooked up to a parachute on the back of the boat. This was about to take me out of my comfort zone, where I had no control of what was about to happen. But the views of the island were spectacular. On this day, I found my courage again. And now that I've done it and enjoyed it, I wouldn't hesitate to do it again. Repetition builds courage.

When I was much younger, stupidity meant doing things that I knew were wrong, yet I did them anyway. When I gained maturity, I realized courage was doing things I knew would benefit me, even if I was scared. Doing things that scare you on a consistent basis, or at least take you out of your comfort zone, will build your muscle of courage a little bit at a time. Courage means you are going to have to take some risks and believe in yourself even when you are so scared. You have to believe that it is all going to turn out okay. Parasailing is one thing. But what does courage look like when the risk is bigger? What if the risk involves changing your life—and your family's lives?

Let me tell you an amazing story of courage about a good friend of mine named Dave. Dave is married with three kids—two grown adults and one young daughter. He was the general manager of a store and had worked there for nearly thirty years. He had grown tired of the corporate life and all the politics that come along with being in upper management, so he started looking at his options and found some franchises that caught his attention. One of these was a new franchise named Kilwins, which is a chocolate and dessert store. Dave did his due diligence to see if this franchise might be a good fit for him and his family. He researched how much money he would need to start out, what kind of location would be necessary in order for him to have the greatest chance of success, and how to hire the right team. For his life to change, he was going to have to quit a well-paying job he'd held for years. This was going to take some serious courage, especially since he is the sole provider for his family.

After deciding on the franchise of Kilwins to be his source of business income, he still had some serious decisions to make since there was no location in his area that would bring him a big enough reward to make this jump. So he started to look outside his community because he knew he would have to have foot traffic walking by the store on a daily basis to make the business work.

Dave finally found a place four hours from where he lived that would be able to provide enough foot traffic for this business to be successful. He decided on Branson, Missouri, and found a building he could lease. In the meantime, he had to find the hundreds of thousands of dollars he needs to make this business happen. Then he had to give his company notice that he would be quitting his job. He put his house on the market. He let his extended family and friends know he was leaving the area. These were just a fraction of the things he had to do to make this massive jump.

Let's talk about five C's of success that Dave had to conquer before making this jump.

> **Clarity**: Dave decided, without a shadow of a doubt, what it was he wanted to do.

> **Competence**: He looked at all his shortcomings and knew he had much to learn in order for him to feel competent enough to start this new franchise, even though most franchises will give you great training using a proven system.

Confidence: I asked Dave if he was nervous and he said he was not. Because of the training (becoming competent) his confidence was very high.

Commitment: When Dave walked into his company's office and told them he was leaving, that was a sure sign of commitment. When he signed the ten-year lease for the new location that was a sure sign of commitment. And when he signed the loan papers for the money he borrowed, that was once again a sure sign of commitment.

Courage: Dave had to have the courage to make a huge change for him and his family. (This is the one item you cannot do without because you can get all the way to the starting line but if you don't have the courage to *actually start*, it was all for nothing. Don't stay stuck on *get ready, get set*, and never *go*.)

Dave and his family's new life started on May 16, 2014, when he opened the doors of his new franchise for the first time. Today he is doing well and is making money, as expected. In some ways it sounds like this change took superhuman strength, but

Dave is just a normal guy who has worked hard all his life. If he can do this, then you can too. So don't ever sell yourself short when it comes to pursuing your dreams.

Remember when I asked you to think back to your own stories of courage? This is what you are going to build on. I cannot tell you enough how important this will be for you to build up yourself through reflecting on the many courageous things you have already done in your life. This is called "logo anchoring" in the psychology world, which is anchoring yourself to stories that empowered you to do courageous things.

Search your heart and life and write down all the things you were scared to do that you actually did. Just be creative here with your list. You will see that deep down inside of you, you already have the courage to accomplish great things—and you've used that same courage in the past. See yourself as the courageous person you need to be in order for you to have the success you want. Your life can be great if you will just have the courage to make that jump across the chasm that is holding you back.

Every time I encounter a big change I need to make, I visualize jumping over a gap between two cliffs. I realize that if I want to reach my goals I am going to have to sometimes jump into the unknown and just trust things will work out. But it's not a totally blind jump—we have planned on things to work out ahead of time before we actually make that jump. This is called taking a calculated risk.

When I started my first business, what gave me the courage to make this huge step into a total world of uncertainty? It was proper planning and preparation. I was working on my business while I was working fulltime. By taking the time to prepare for the launch of my first business I was building my courage, my confidence, and my competence. The commitment came the day I gave my company notice I was quitting. I would have never had the courage to do this without a great support system from my wife and kids, and me taking the time to prepare myself for battle.

Speaking of battle, do you think the military just sends soldiers into battle before they have prepared them to do what is required of them on the battlefield? Look at the amount of time they spend in just basic training. They will spend around thirteen weeks just preparing to be a *basic* soldier. This will give them the courage to do basic things using a support system in whatever battle they are thrown into. So they have courage to do above normal things from the average human being. How do they increase their courage again well they go through specialized training which is to help them increase their clarity, competence, confidence, commitment, and especially courage? When they are focusing on the five C's to success, they will automatically be courageous when on the battlefield.

Just like a soldier, your courage can be developed over time if you will just make the time to develop it. As long as you wait on it to come to you, you will spend the rest of your life waiting. Courage is something you will have to *go after*. You have to make creating courage in your life and absolute must, as this is what's going to keep you going when the going gets tough.

Many times I have wanted to throw in the towel, but I always look back at the ways I have overcome obstacles and use those as anchors to keep me going. Your courage anchors are going to be one of your greatest resources you will ever have. You know what an anchor does, don't you? It keeps you from floating away. Courage is the one thing that may just keep you going and keep you steady in tough times.

Take the time to develop the muscle of courage and your success is sure to come. With courage you will be able to overcome and conquer anything. It will help you to take the appropriate educated risks in order to achieve your goals. Never give up; just keep focusing on the solution.

Notes:

"Keep going, keep going, and keep going, I say just keep going." ~ *Eric Rios*

Chapter 6

Getting and Staying Motivated

You're going to need this to climb to your highest level.

Now that you have defined what it is you want, you have reached an adequate level of competence, your confidence is up enough for you to get started, you have made a commitment to get started, and you have found the courage you need to open that great door to the most rewarding life you have ever imagined, you are going to need something to help you get motivated and stay motivated. This is extremely important—your level of motivation will determine how far you will go in your journey of life.

Have you ever asked yourself what it is that motivates you? Many things in my own life keep me motivated. Once I was as broke as broke could be; now I use this as a motivator. Being able to provide for my kids helps me to stay motivated. I use my desire to succeed as a motivator. Some people will need a ton of leverage to get going and keep going toward their goals. For others, it may take just a small amount of motivation to get yourself going. As for me, it took seeing what and where my life was and where I wanted to be. Once I knew what I wanted, it was easy for me to make the jump from an employee to a new business owner. Once I figured out what I wanted, I was motivated to spend the necessary time getting to know everything about the journey I was about to embark on. Once I had taken the time to become a competent business owner, I automatically developed the other traits necessary to make my jump into the land of entrepreneurship. When I quit my job and started a business without even one customer, I put myself in a place where I had no choice but to succeed. That's what I call leverage. When you close the door behind you, you have only one choice and that is to keep moving forward to success.

Things may get really hard and thoughts of giving up may cross your mind many times. Remember, these are just thoughts and you have control over what thoughts you allow to stay in your mind. If you have a good support system, allow them to help keep you motivated. My wife has been one of my greatest supports in keeping me motivated when things have been tough. I am a very proud person when it comes to sharing my personal feelings, especially with my wife. I feel that I am supposed to be the strong one and not show my weaknesses—at least this is what I tell myself sometimes. However, I have learned that trusting my wife to help me stay motivated has been one of the most rewarding things in my life. She is the rock I can count on to give me the encouragement I need to keep going.

I have also spent much of my time trusting in God and living by faith. I have always said that if you want to learn to live by faith, you should start a business! I have trusted God with my life and business and trusted my wife to make sure I had the encouragement to keep me going. I have also found that my accountant has been so amazing in keeping me encouraged. If I was down because business was slow, Jason would get out the financials and start showing me just how successful we have been as a company. That provides me so much support just by showing me where we were and how far we have come as a business. Early on, when I started the business, I grew just a little too fast, which is a great problem to have, but it caused me to become a cash-strapped business. Still, I was determined and was able to stay motivated. I found ways to generate the necessary funds to keep me going.

An avid student of excellence, Anthony Robbins has been an amazing inspiration in my life, causing me to work hard on myself and showing me that great things can happen if you will just try. Brian Tracy's messages, especially from his *Crunch Time!* program also kept me going so many times when things were hard.

This CD, about how and when to make the business decisions, has kept me making so many of the right decisions more than anything I have ever listened to or read.

Once, when I hired a business coaching company, the coach assigned to me told me very bluntly that if I was not going to listen to what he told me to do, then I might as well not waste my money—twenty-five thousand dollars for a year of training. By following the instructions that were given to me by the business coach, I watched our company's revenue *double* over the next year. We hit a million dollars in revenue the day before Thanksgiving. This was a monumental moment for me. I had never attended college, and hadn't even finished high school, but I was now running a million-dollar company. A business coach can be a lifesaver, if you will are willing to listen to what he or she has to say.

Another one of my favorite authors, Norman Vincent Peale, was such an inspiration to me. His book, *The Power of Positive Thinking,* helped me make sure I kept my perspective on the right things by staying positive and seeing the good in every bad deal I faced. That book is a life changer for most who read and apply what they learn in the book. Norman was a preacher and completely trusted God with his life, and like me, he had an amazing wife who was a great support for him. There times when he went to his wife feeling down because his life was seemingly falling apart. She would remind him about what God had done in his life before and for him to put his trust in the One who has helped him do the things he needed to get done on other occasions.

I think you can agree that getting motivated and staying motivated is going to be one of the most important things you can do in your life. You really are going to need to take some time to write down all of the things you think will get you motivated and those things that will keep you motivated. You have likely heard the saying “Those who fail to plan, plan to fail.” So if you can preplan your motivators, you will be able to work smarter, longer, and accomplish more because every time something happens, you already have a plan to get and stay motivated to go another round in the ring.

Many boxers keep a picture of their opponent in full view during training as a motivator before they step into the ring. They will use this as the fuel to keep them going to make sure they are preparing themselves to win this fight. We can use similar things to keep us motivated as well. Find a picture of something that keeps fueling your fire and keep it in front of you every day. The more things you can use to keep you going the more motivated you will stay. No boxer ever goes into the ring with an opponent without studying the opponent first—the fighter studies every weakness and every strength. Just like a boxer, you want to go into that ring with every bit of knowledge about the challenges you will face.

Have you ever noticed that in every boxer's corner is someone who is coaching and motivating him to make the right choices and keep going no matter how hard it gets? Those who have planned tend to always have a much better chance of success when they are facing an enormous challenge—they plan to have someone in their corner. So what are you going to do starting right now to plan and prepare for the challenge at hand and for the future challenges you will possibly face?

The average business faces some kind of crisis around four times a year. Hearing this statistic helped me to see my business through a different lens; it helped to make better decisions based on someone else's experiences. But also it made me look ahead at the possible problems I might face before they ever arose. This has been one of the greatest assets in keeping me motivated by always feeding my mind with the right information from the right people or resources.

So what are you going to do with what you have now learned? Have you started a new list of all the things it is going to take you to get motivated and stay motivated? I want you to make this a priority. Make sure you take this list of motivators you have created and put it everywhere you will be throughout your day. This means in your car, on your bathroom mirror, on your desk at work, on your desk at home, and I mean anywhere you can to make sure you are constantly reminding yourself to get done what you need to get done. Don't wait until you have everything just right either, because this day will never come. Just get moving and get moving now.

I once met a guy that was a financial guru and could easily make a lot of money in his field of work. He had a desire to start a business, but was so scared to do so at a ripe old age that he was at still stuck working in a job that was less than satisfying. He was able to find every reason not to start the business he told me he wanted to start. I felt bad for him as we parted ways, because I knew he wouldn't ever make the jump. I hate seeing people give up so easily on their dreams. But you don't have to be another statistic in this world! Look at the life of Nelson Mandela. He believed in something so strongly—equal rights for all the people in Africa—that he was willing to do whatever it took to see this through. He spent many years in prison and became an old man there before his political dreams of equality were realized and he became the president of his country.

We can sit around and make every excuse in the world, but if you're not willing to get started, all you are doing is cheating yourself and others. So many people can benefit from your great talents if you can just find something to get you motivated and keep you motivated. Plan your motivators in advance, and you will find that things will go so much more smoothly. Some people will call this getting a mastermind group, which is a group of people who are going to help you stay motivated and hold you accountable to reaching your goals. Get busy doing something every day towards your dream life. Yes, it is going to be scary. Yes, it is going to be hard. You are going to have setbacks. You are going to question why you even made such a decision. But more than that, you are going to have so many glorious successes that you will be able to celebrate on a regular basis. Eventually you will have more successes than you will failures. In fact, for every failure you will have *two successes*. I say that because every time you do something right, that's a success. And everything you do something wrong and learn from it, that's a success. So, in reality, there is no such thing as *failure* if you are always learning from each mistake.

Notes:

"Celebrate what you have accomplished but raise the bar a little higher each time you succeed."

~ Mia Hamm

Chapter 7

Success Breeds Success

How to use your wins as anchors.

One thing I find that keeps an individual working toward his or her goals and dreams is building on each success. Sometimes all we seem to see are the failures we have had in this life, and not all the little successes we have had. I have created *more* challenges for myself because I could not see past my mistakes and failures. That's all I would focus on and let it dominate my thoughts, which it caused it to dominate my actions. When your thoughts are on the wrong things, your actions are sure to follow.

In this chapter, we're going to talk about how *success breeds success*. But we're also going to talk about how *failure breeds failure*. What we focus on is the direction we tend to go. A ship that has set its course on a destination will automatically work toward that destination. So the real question for you is, what are you focusing on? Are you focusing on your failures, or are you focusing on your successes? Which one is a greater motivator?

Have you ever taken the time to think about what you are being motivated to do? What are you are doing on a daily basis? Are you working toward what you want or are you running from what you want? Are you seeing yourself being the person you so desperately want to be or do see yourself being the person you despise?

During hard times, we will get into one of two different funks—either the one that leads us to where we want to be, or the one that is leading us down the road we hate. The problem with being motivated by our failures is that they keep us moving in the opposite direction of our dreams and goals.

I stated that success breeds success and failure breeds failure, but what does this really mean? When all you focus on are your failures and mistakes, you will only reproduce those same actions. When you focus on all of your successes, no matter how big and small, and use your failures as stepping-stones to climb up the ladder of success, then and only then are you reproducing success.

One of the best ways to start focusing and building on all of the successes you have and have accomplished is to look back over the list you made in chapter five of everything you have ever done right—all of your successes. This is where you are going to anchor all of your thoughts while you are on your journey of building the dream life you desire. You are going to go back to every success you have ever had and you are going to use these as your catapult to get where you want. Don't limit yourself to what you write down for your own successes. As you read over the list, look at every part of your life, starting back from the first memory you have of doing something right. Look at the first A you got in school, look at the first sporting event you won, look at the first excellent meal you ever made, look at the time when you got a promotion at work.

If you're married, you can also ask your spouse to write down every successful thing you have ever done. I asked my wife to do this, and it was pretty amazing to see the different things I has been successful in that I did not even think about. This really changed my perspective on where I was and how I was really doing in my current life. I also asked myself a lot of questions:

What one thing do I want to do in life that I am afraid to do?

What one thing do I really want to do, knowing no matter what, I cannot fail?

What one thing do I want to do that scares me the most?

What one thing do I want to do but have put it off because I don't think it is possible to achieve?

What one thing would change my life, yet I have done nothing to work toward it because I didn't have the courage to get started?

What one thing have I made every excuse in the world not to do?

Your life will change when you put this amazing process into action. When you do this, things are going to get interesting.

By now you should have already made long list of your successes, both big and small, (and remember this list can be *anything* you have done that you felt you have done right—as small as learning to play an instrument or learning how to play a simple card game). All of these items are going to be your building blocks and successes you build on to get to your dream.

One of the smartest things an individual can do is to track where they started to where they are today, so let's jog your memory a little here. If you are thinking to yourself, "I had nothing to write down," here are some common things that most people will automatically overlook when it comes to their own lives:

Success # 1 – You got a good grade on a test.

Success # 2 – You completed a project on time.

Success # 3 – You learned a new skill.

Success # 4 – You learned how to tie your shoe in record time.

Success # 5 – You taught your dog how to sit.

Success # 6 – You learned how to walk.

Success # 7 – You learned a new language.

Success # 8 – You programmed a remote control to a TV.

Success # 9 – You started a club of some kind.

Success # 10 – You made someone smile.

This is a very simple list of successes a person could have had in their life, but if you are climbing a ladder and you are using all of your small successes to build on, you are likely now *ten steps higher* than when you started. It doesn't matter how big the success is, it just matters that you use your successes to build on.

Maybe you closed a million-dollar deal. You might have invented something that changed someone's life. You might have reached an enormous goal you thought was impossible. Each of these successes are stepping stones, or rungs, on a ladder to help you get where you want to go, which is up. Nobody in his or her right mind wants to go *down* the ladder. Yet you would be surprised how many people seem to work harder at going downhill than they do trying to go uphill. This sounds crazy, doesn't it? But they are doing this every day without realizing this is where life is going. This is called being unaware of where you are.

Imagine driving down the street unaware of where you are or where you are going. This would be the most chaotic and interesting ride of your life, not to mention a very fruitless effort. When our self-image or self-esteem is not congruent with our goals, it will almost be impossible for us to reach our goals. You have to have a positive self-image, or self-esteem, if you are going to get where you want to be. You have got to believe in yourself with such passion that nothing will be able to stop you. This is where your list of successes will come in handy. When you have stopped believing in yourself, go to your list of small and large successes and just see how awesome you really are.

Imagine climbing up on the shoulders of a giant; imagine what you are now able to see that you were not able to see before. Let's say the great Warren Buffet came over to your house and said he wants to share his most successful stories on how he became successful. You would all of a sudden be automatically given a helicopter ride to the top of the ladder, because you are now building on the success of a giant. When extremely successful people share their successes, you need to make sure you are listening to everything they have to say, as this is going to be the lift you will need to get you where you want to be.

I always look at who has been successful in what it is I want to do, and I learn everything there is about what and how they have done it. I take this information and use it as a catapult to get where I want to be. I use their successes to build upon, even if it costs me tens of thousands of dollars, on learning materials such as books, audio CDs, DVDs, seminars, and coaching to get to where I am today.

Make today the day you decide to build upon your successes and the successes of others to help you get where you want to be. Go find everything and anyone who will share how they did it and eliminate many years of heartache for yourself. Because when you build on your successes and the success of others, you will bypass many rungs on the ladder. Don't be too proud to ask for help, and don't be too arrogant to not realize there is always possibly a better way. Let your greatness shine for the world to see. Let your time here on this earth be the best possible time ever. Share all of your greatness with everyone who you come across. This is where the great rewards of life come from.

I have found that when I am sharing my own successful stories with others, it is so inspiring to both parties. Likewise, I *love* hearing about the successes in other people's lives because it always leaves me with a different perspective, a new appreciation, or some new information I didn't have before.

Please, make knowing your successes and sharing them an important part of your life. You would be shocked to know how many people would love to just hear your story of greatness, whether it's a successful marriage, a successful business startup, or graduating from college at an older age. Sometimes the greatest stories of success are from people who didn't achieve it quickly, but kept working toward their goals over many years.

My wife has one of those amazing stories of success. She spent almost twenty years getting her college degree after she graduated from high school. She did a little bit at a time while she worked a fulltime job, but she stayed with it until she graduated with her degree in business. She made this a priority, even after being married and having kids to raise. Inspiring!

Every person can share their stories of greatness with others who will be encouraged to live a life of greatness.

Notes:

"Procrastination is the bad habit of putting off until the day after tomorrow what should have been done the day before yesterday."

~ Napoleon Hill

Chapter 8

Parting Ways with Procrastination

Avoid the number-one killer of all dreams.

Putting things off is the number-one killer of anything you ever set out to do. We're so good at procrastination that we can sometimes disguise it as "being busy." How do I know this? I guarantee that you can sit down right now and make a *giant list* of things you have put off, instead of *actually doing those things* that could potentially make a huge difference in your life. Keeping a list may seem to be helpful to your cause—and maybe it truly is if you're using a list to visualize what you need to do, and you systematically check off each item as you do it. However, some people use list-making as a form of procrastination. They'll make a list and rearrange it ten times but they won't actually tackle any of the items on it. I know without a doubt that this kind of "busy procrastination" is killing so many dreams right now, because of all the reasons you can find to procrastinate about what you want to do. Don't wait until it is too late and you no longer have the ability to reach your goal.

Procrastination kills your chances of ever having anything worthwhile. If you don't slay this giant now, it is going to take everything you have ever dreamed of having. You have to make it a daily habit of destroying the habit of procrastination. This is a bad habit, just like smoking. It even has some really bad side effects that you don't notice over long period of time, yet your inaction will eventually be what destroys your hopes and dreams. If you can't make stomping out procrastination an absolute priority, you will find yourself looking back, wishing you would have taken the time to do the things you really wanted to do. Don't look back on your life with regret for the things you did not do because of the disease of procrastination!

If your doctor came to you and said you have a major illness and it is going to kill you in a few short years, you would probably start looking at your life in a different way. It's a morbid example, but it happens every day. I have seen people who were dying all of a sudden start living a very different life based on what the doctor has told them. They start making life an absolute priority each day because they now realize that this precious life they have may be gone very soon.

Well, pretend I am the doctor, standing before you today, telling you that you have this horrendous disease called procrastination, and it is killing your life's dreams, your physical health, your mental health, and your spiritual health. If you've ever stepped on the scale and regretted your eating habits, you likely know that losing a few extra pounds, or walking a mile or so a day, could help your health. It could even save your life. Likewise, if you knew that having certain priorities in your life would make your life better, then I think it is obvious that it would benefit you do them consistently. And if you don't do those things, it might just get worse.

Think about this for a moment and ask yourself right now, am I putting things off I know I should be doing that could make my life better? Am I not doing the things that I know could make my family's life better? Am I working against myself by putting off the important things in my life? Am I not taking my daily medicine that kills the disease called procrastination?

Now that you have answered some of the questions above, ask yourself this question: why am I procrastinating? Is it due to fear? Is it due to a lack of knowledge? When you understand *why* something is happening, it offers you the opportunity to see how it can be overcome. If you are putting something off because of fear, then you need to look yourself, why am I scared to do this thing I want to do?

Let's say you are auditioning for a part in a theatrical play, but you keep finding yourself not studying the lines because you feel as though you don't have what it takes to get in front of a big crowd. You are afraid to get up in front of them because you are afraid you will be a big flop. So you keep finding excuses not to study your lines so they will be sure not to call you up on the stage to do the part. You are using fear as your excuse to put off studying, even though you know it is the *most important thing* you could be doing right now. This is where you have to have your courage muscle working for you. If you have been doing the things you need to do to grow that courage muscle, then we should be getting past the fears that are causing us to procrastinate.

The Fear Factor

Fear can cause us to not really live. For many years I thought I was an invincible and indestructible individual and could not be hurt—until the day that would change my life forever. I was thirty-four years old and was playing soccer on an indoor field. I was a very fast runner and an aggressive player. I had always believed that you could make up for a lack of skill with being aggressive. During one play, I was running full speed toward the soccer ball with no one close to me and when I stopped to turn I heard a big pop and I fell down onto the ground. I had just torn my meniscus and ACL. For the first time in my life, I had a serious injury I would not be able to just get up and walk away from.

This injury began a downhill slide for me for the next couple of years because I finally came to the conclusion that I was not indestructible and was not going to live forever. I don't know why this bothered me as much as it did, but this injury would become a defining moment for me. I suffered major anxiety from this injury and the feelings and thoughts it sparked. I got the knee fixed, but after that I became depressed and fought anxiety, which I had never experienced before. Before, I was invincible. Now I was afraid to live for the first time in my life. I ended up allowing this to affect so much of my life, both personal and professional.

I turned in my company vehicle, stopped going to work for a short time, and stopped going to the everyday places I had been going to for the last thirty years. This anxiety was really taking a toll on my life in every way imaginable; it had created such a fear in me that it prohibited me from functioning as a normal human being. I visited a couple different therapists but found no relief. My doctor wanted to put me on drugs to calm me down, but I was stubborn and wanted to find a real solution that did not treat the symptom of the problem but the actual problem itself. There was no time for procrastination in my life if I was going to overcome my enormous fear. This sent me on the quest of studying everything there was about the problem of anxiety. While my anxiety did subside, I also gained something even more valuable—I had studied so much to overcome my fears that I became a lover of education and learning! It turned into an avid and voracious reader.

Once I started living my life on purpose, I no longer let obstacles stop me. Instead I'd think about every way I could overcome a problem. The pain that created so much fear in my life ended up being what propelled me forward. Like so many, we find every excuse in the world to put things off until it is either too late or something drastic happens. We put off applying for that job because we are afraid we don't have enough experience, or we are afraid we don't have the proper amount of education. We use fear as an excuse not to talk to a man or woman we find very attractive. We use this fear to put off living an extraordinary life. So we procrastinate (put off what we know we should do, even though doing those things might that just bring about something amazing if we only tried).

People who are bold in their actions and make the habit of taking action, no matter what the outcome, are the ones who live the most fulfilled lives. Remember the list we talked about earlier in this chapter—how some people use it to get things done and some people use it to procrastinate? Here's where it counts as actual work and not procrastination. Make a complete list of things you know you've put off that you should be doing. Now, keep in mind that this is not a list of your normal household chores, but rather a list of items that can have a great impact on your life being better or worse.

After you've made the first list, put the items in order from the most important at the top to the least important at the bottom. Now take that newly rearranged list and write out what you think will be the easiest to start doing, from the top down, to the most difficult item you know you need to do. Start with the simplest item first. If it can be completed in one session of effort (like doing laundry or writing out thank-you cards), do it today. If it will require a longer period off time, do this for a minimum of thirty days every single day at the exact same time. No matter how large the list is, just do one item at a time for a month and cross the items off as you go. This is going to help you start to develop a habit of doing those things you have put off, and it will also build your confidence so when you start the harder tasks they no longer seem so hard anymore. You will start creating new habits in a very simple way that does not seem impossible.

We talked earlier about how success builds on success. This is the same principle that you will use. Complete the easy items first as a way to start building your confidence and gradually build on that. If you see you have been putting something off that has the ability to change your life *right now*, this is the thing you need to do right now—even if it seems like you just can't do it. Do it right now, or put some effort toward it at this very moment. Say you're mad at someone—so mad that you have been losing sleep over your negative feelings toward them. You know if you talk to them, you may feel better, but because of your anger you don't do it, so you keep living in anger. Is it really worth your sleep habits, thought patterns, and overall health to hold a grudge? Chances are, you're the only one losing sleep over the issue. Best to face it head on and resolve the situation.

When the obstacle before you is serious, you have to make it a priority. If it is urgent, you have to make it a priority or the opportunity to overcome and move forward may just go away. Many opportunities have been presented to people that have later been removed because some form of action was never taken to secure that opportunity. We have used the excuse of procrastination for so long and have labeled ourselves as procrastinators that we make sure we do everything in our power to *live down* to that label we have given ourselves. If you don't believe this, just look back over the last five years or ten years and ask yourself if you would have made different decisions would your life have been different. If you would have made the decisions you knew you should have made, how different could your life have been? How different *can it still be* if you start now?

We get a great opportunity to write our own story and create our own lives. We can make our lives exactly what we want them to be, if we can first just decide what it is we want our lives to be like, then put the necessary steps into action to secure our future the way we have envisioned it to be. Procrastination is just a word. It only has power over us if we allow it to have power over us. Starting right now, you have the power to destroy this enemy by taking some kind of action, no matter how small.

Notes:

Notes

"Today I begin a new life. Today I shed my old skin which hath, too long, suffered the bruises of failure and the wounds of mediocrity. Today I am born anew and my birthplace is a vineyard where there is a fruit for all." *~ Og Mandino*

Chapter 9

Embracing the New You

Create your ideal life.

Creating your new life means you get to start over—creating your life and not having someone else creating a life for you. Your life matters so much, as do the lives of your family and friends. If you could just live every part of your life on purpose, I promise your life can be so much different. The day I started living my life on purpose and no longer just existing I found so much peace in living.

The problem with so many of us is we get to the point of knowing what's next for us but really make no effort to apply what will be next in our lives. We have spent time on learning everything we want to do, but we don't really make the necessary effort to do what is next. What's next is simple. You can start now—this very moment—to work toward what you have decided on what it is you want to do. Many people have a college degree of some kind and are doing nothing with the degree they spent so much time and money on accumulating. They spent years getting this or that specialty degree, but are still working in doing something that really does not drive them or bring out their inner passion.

I once met a woman who had spent the last seven years going to college for a specialty degree in sports management, but she was not doing anything with her degree. Instead, she was working in the office of a company in a field completely unrelated to what she wanted to do. When I asked her if she was using any of her skills that she had learned in college, she said no. I asked her what her dream job was and she said to work in a specific sports team's front office. I asked her if she had ever sent in a resume to this organization and she said no. She had just spent *seven years* in college learning a very specific skill so she could work in a very specific environment, but had never made any effort of any kind to work at her dream job. This blows me away!

You have to say yes to the possible opportunities in front of you if you are ever going to live your dream. It takes courage to make yourself do that one thing you might be rejected for. But if you don't try, you will truly never know if you could have the job of your dreams. I tell people that, "You get one hundred percent of what you don't ask for." If you don't step in the direction of your dream, then you will only be helping someone else fulfill their dream. You may never regret the things you have done, but you will surely regret the things you did not do. You have to at least try or you will live a complete life of disappointment. Stop making excuses, throw everything you have at your dream, and see what sticks.

One evening I walked into an ice cream shop and started a conversation with a young high school student that was behind the counter. She was a senior in high school, so I asked her what her plan was when she left school. She said she wanted to be a psychologist. She then began to tell me all the reasons as to why she may not do it because she said the market has so many of them already and she could not see how she would be able to get a job doing this. I was shocked that she had already closed the door on her dream based on what she only *thought she might be able to do.* I began to talk to her about all the great opportunities she would have if she became a psychologist. I shared with her that the sky would be the limit for her and gave her different ideas about how she could be successful. Getting her to think was a key factor in changing her perception about what she wanted to do.

Sometimes it only takes us thinking for a moment about what *could be* and trying to analyze what opportunities are really out there for us. When I left that little ice cream shop, she was so excited and ready to move forward with her life of becoming a psychologist and living her dream life. I told her I was going to drop off a copy of one of my favorite CD sets by Jim Rohn called, *The Challenge to Succeed*. By the time my wife dropped this off to her, she was worked up and excited to go do something with her life. All it took was some encouragement and a different perspective to allow her to change her perception of what she thought was possible or impossible.

Taking action is what you have to do if you are ever going to get where you want to be. No matter how much education you get, it will not be enough to get you where you want to be. In order for you to make this work, you have to take action. When you shortchange yourself because you are afraid and procrastinate, you will look back on your life with regret. Remember the race always goes to the one who takes action.

Some people want a job that pays a certain amount of money, but are really not sure as to what jobs pay that amount of money. I suggest that you go online and research all the jobs that you have an interest in. I also suggest that you start with how much money you would like to make, it can give you a head start in finding what you want by knowing what certain jobs pay.

You also have to be willing to pay the price to have the career you want. Some career fields will require you paying an enormous price for the necessary education. I want you to consider the cost before you invest time and money. You can always make your money back, but your time is the only thing you will never get back in your life. You need to really value your time and not waste it.

As you review the list and the income estimates, don't let this information deter you from what you want to do. Some of these positions can be attained without an education or the financial investment. Not all, of course, but some. There are plenty of people who don't have a college degree but who are doing very well, so only use this as a guide to discover how many options are available in the workforce.

At this point, it is a good idea to define how much money you want to make for your career. You can see if the career you have chosen matches how money you want to make in your life. So as you go through the list of career fields, I want you to think about what you're passionate about and decide on a career that will make you so excited every day to get out of that bed and hit the ground running. This career needs to make you smile when you think about it. It needs to make you feel all giddy inside when you think about it. If you have a set amount of income you'd like to make, see if your chosen career matches up there too.

You don't want to spend your life doing something that you will be unhappy doing. You might have some unhappy jobs while you are working on acquiring the skills you need to have the career you desire to have, but those jobs should not be your end result—this is just the beginning to your dream life. Your dream can come true if you will just work towards it. But you have to at least work towards it.

Imagine taking a cruise—you've paid a bunch of money to visit some remote amazing destination, but the ship decides not to chart a course to that destination. Wouldn't you feel ripped off if you got to the wrong destination? This is the same thing with your life. If you don't chart a course toward where you want to go, you will end up very disappointed with where you end up.

Life does not have to be tough if you will just decide on what you want to do. When you decide what you want, this will be so much simpler for you. If you need to, go back through the book and read the chapters on clarity, competence, confidence, commitment, and courage. Make sure you apply them to what you are doing and you will find your success to be a much simpler process.

Now go and get busy deciding what life you will create. Let your light shine so the rest of the world can have the same hope you have. You were created in the image of God and His likeness, so let yourself shine in the greatness He has given you. Live your life to the fullest and watch your dreams come true!

Notes:

Notes

Appendix

Game-Changing Books

A list of impactful books and audio programs for those who want to change their lives.

Everyone in their life will need some kind of help in achieving their own greatness. No has ever achieved greatness in their lives without the help of someone else. This help could have come from many different areas and many different individuals. I have compiled a list of books and audio programs that I have personally used in my own life over the last ten years that helped shape my life into an extraordinary life. I want you to look through some of the categories that I have listed that you want to excel at in your own life. When you find the resource go out and get that book or audio program and turn into a life changing tool for creating your own greatness. I have spent thousands of dollars on programs that I have included here so make sure you go through the areas that you are struggling with and take some massive action on accomplishing what you want out of your life.

I've mentioned many books that I have read that have changed my own life in so many ways. Below is a list of my favorite and most impactful books and audio programs that I suggest to anyone wanting to learn how to change their lives. For almost any area of your life—from anxiety to business—I believe the knowledge within these books can change your life and help you achieve your own greatness.

Business

If you are to go into business you are going to need some help. No business has ever succeeded without the help of other people or organizations. I have shared with you some of my most treasured books that I have read on business. For me these are treasures, as I have never had a normal formal education. Take the time to check them out and look for the ones that fit your needs at this time and learn from them.

Midas Touch: Why Some Entrepreneurs Get Rich—And Why Most Don't by Donald J. Trump and Robert T. Kiyosaki

Internet Prophets: The World's Leading Experts Reveal How to Profit Online by Steve Olsher

Trump: The Art of the Deal by Donald J. Trump and Tony Schwartz

Have a Great Year Every Year: A Four-Point Program for Maximizing Your Performance by Dave Yoho

The 4-Hour Workweek: Escape 9-5, Live Anywhere, and Join the New Rich by Timothy Ferriss

The Pumpkin Plan: A Simple Strategy to Grow a Remarkable Business in Any Field by Mike Michalowicz

Service Failure: The Real Reasons Employees Struggle With Customer Service and What You Can Do About It by Jeff Toister

How to Write a Business Plan (Creating Success) by Brian Finch

Good to Great: Why Some Companies Make the Leap . . . And Others Don't by Jim Collins

Put Your Dream to the Test: 10 Questions to Help You See It and Seize It by John C. Maxwell

Built to Last: Successful Habits of Visionary Companies by Jim Collins and Jerry I. Porras

"I Got Here. You Can Too!" A Masters Course in Becoming a Millionaire by Bruce A. Berman

Profit First: A Simple System to Transform Any Business from a Cash-Eating Monster to a Money-Making Machine by Mike Michalowicz

Whale Done!: The Power of Positive Relationships by Kenneth Blanchard and Thad Lacinak

The Brian Tracy Success Library: *Time Management, Motivation, Delegation & Supervision,* and *Negotiation*, all by Brian Tracy

Warren Buffett's Management Secrets: Proven Tools for Personal and Business Success by Mary Buffett and David Clark

Like a Virgin: Secrets They Won't Teach You at Business School by Richard Branson

Who Moved My Cheese?: An A-Mazing Way to Deal with Change in Your Work and in Your Life by Spencer Johnson and Kenneth Blanchard

The One Minute Manager by Kenneth Blanchard and Spencer Johnson

The Five Most Important Questions You Will Ever Ask About Your Organization by Peter F. Drucker and Leader to Leader Institute (Formerly The Drucker Foundation)

Who Killed Change?: Solving the Mystery of Leading People Through Change by Ken Blanchard and John Britt

Leadership and the One Minute Manager Updated Ed: Increasing Effectiveness Through Situational Leadership II by Ken Blanchard, Patricia Zigarmi, and Drea Zigarmi

Business Adventures: Twelve Classic Tales from the World of Wall Street by John Brooks

Raving Fans: A Revolutionary Approach To Customer Service by Ken Blanchard and Sheldon Bowles

The Toilet Paper Entrepreneur: The tell-it-like-it-is guide to cleaning up in business, even if you are at the . . . by Mike Michalowicz and HarperCo Books

The Hero and the Outlaw: Building Extraordinary Brands Through the Power of Archetypes by Margaret Mark and Carol Pearson

Make Money in Real Estate Tax Liens: How To Guarantee Your Return Up To 50% by Chantal Howell Carey and Bill Carey

Pour Your Heart Into It: How Starbucks Built a Company One Cup at a Time by Howard Schultz and Dori jones Yang

The Rules of Work: The Unspoken Truth About Getting Ahead in Business by Richard Templar

Success!: The Glenn Bland Method by Glenn Bland

Love 'Em or Lose 'Em: Getting Good People to Stay by Beverly Kaye and Sharon Jordan-Evans

22 Success Lessons From Baseball by Ron White

Acres of Diamonds (Life-Changing Classics) by Russell H. Conwell and John Wanamaker

The Rules of Management, Expanded Edition: A Definitive Code for Managerial Success (Richard Templar's Rules) by Richard Templar

Finance & Financial Mindset

Sometimes in order to understand, we need to make sure we are learning from the most brilliant minds available. When you take the time to read a book on finance or just financial mindset, this one act all by itself can be a game changer for you.

The Master Key to Riches by Napoleon Hill

How to Read and Understand Financial Statements When You Don't Know What You Are Looking At: For Business Owners and Investors by Brian Kline

Leap: Lifetime Economic Acceleration Process by Robert Castiglione

How to Read a Financial Report: Wringing Vital Signs Out of the Numbers by John A. Tracy and Tage Tracy

Financial Statements: A Step-by-Step Guide to Understanding and Creating Financial Reports by Thomas R. Ittelson

Becoming a Millionaire God's Way: Getting Money to You, Not from You by Dr. C. Thomas Anderson

Retire Young Retire Rich: How to Get Rich Quickly and Stay Rich Forever! (Rich Dad's series) by Robert T. Kiyosaki

MONEY Master the Game: 7 Simple Steps to Financial Freedom by Tony Robbins

Rich Dad's Guide to Investing: What the Rich Invest in, That the Poor and Middle Class Do Not! by Robert T. Kiyosaki

A Path to Financial Peace of Mind by Dwayne Burnell

Start Late, Finish Rich: A No-Fail Plan for Achieving Financial Freedom at Any Age (Finish Rich series) by David Bach

Unfair Advantage: The Power of Financial Education by Robert T. Kiyosaki

The Science of Getting Rich: Attracting Financial Success through Creative Thought by Wallace D. Wattles

Rich Dad's Conspiracy of the Rich: The 8 New Rules of Money by Robert T. Kiyosaki

Rich Dad's CASHFLOW Quadrant: Rich Dad's Guide to Financial Freedom by Robert T. Kiyosaki

Profit First: A Simple System to Transform Any Business from a Cash-Eating Monster to a Money-Making Machine by Mike Michalowicz

Rich Dad's Prophecy: Why the Biggest Stock Market Crash in History is Still Coming by Robert T. Kiyosaki and Sharon L. Lechter

You're Broke Because You Want to Be: How to Stop Getting By and Start Getting Ahead by Larry Winget

Leadership

I have come to realize that without leadership you can only go so far. If you are ever to accomplish much, you will need to raise your leadership abilities. You or your business will only grow to your leadership level. If you want to excel, then you need to raise your leadership abilities.

Self Leadership and the One Minute Manager: Increasing Effectiveness Through Situational Self Leadership by Ken Blanchard and Susan Fowler

The Leadership Pill: The Missing Ingredient in Motivating People Today by Kenneth Blanchard and Marc Muchnick

Inspire! What Great Leaders Do by Lance Secretan

No B.S. Time Management for Entrepreneurs: The Ultimate No Holds Barred Kick Butt Take No Prisoners Guide to Time Productivity and Sanity by Dan S. Kennedy

Tribal Leadership: Leveraging Natural Groups to Build a Thriving Organization by Dave Logan, John King, and Halee Fischer-Wright

The Discipline of Market Leaders: Choose Your Customers, Narrow Your Focus, Dominate Your Market by Michael Treacy and Fred Wiersema

Leadership and the One Minute Manager: Increasing Effectiveness Through Situational Leadership by Ken Blanchard, Patricia Zigarmi, and Drea Zigarmi

The 360 Degree Leader: Developing Your Influence from Anywhere in the Organization by John C. Maxwell

Developing the Leaders Around You: How to Help Others Reach Their Full Potential by John C. Maxwell

Leadership (The Brian Tracy Success Library) by Brian Tracy

Whale Done!: The Power of Positive Relationships by Kenneth Blanchard PhD, Thad Lacinak, Chuck Tompkins, and Jim Ballard

The Secret: What Great Leaders Know and Do by Ken Blanchard and Mark Miller

The Way of the SEAL: Think Like an Elite Warrior to Lead and Succeed Hardcover by Mark Divine and Allyson E. Machate

Management (The Brian Tracy Success Library) by Brian Tracy

The 21 Irrefutable Laws of Leadership: Follow Them and People Will Follow You by John Maxwell

Marketing

The key to any successful business or personal adventure is the ability to market yourself to any and everyone who you come across. Marketing can make or break your business. If you can't get this right, you very well might not make it in doing great things. Use this list of marketing resources to get your marketing groove on and change your life and the lives of others.

Marketing (The Brian Tracy Success Library) by Brian Tracy

All Marketers Are Liars: The Underground Classic that Explains How Marketing Really Works—and Why Authenticity Is the Best Marketing of All by Seth Godin

Purple Cow: Transform Your Business by Being Remarkable by Seth Godin

The Big Moo: Stop Trying to Be Perfect and Start Being Remarkable by The Group of 33 and Seth Godin

Selling the Invisible: A Field Guide to Modern Marketing by Harry Beckwith

Guerrilla Marketing on the Front Lines: 35 World-Class Strategies to Send Your Profits Soaring by Jay Conrad Levinson and Mitch Meyerson

The Ultimate Marketing Plan: Target Your Audience! Get Out Your Message! Build Your Brand!
by Dan S. Kennedy

No B.S. Direct Marketing: The Ultimate No Holds Barred Kick Butt Take No Prisoners Direct Marketing for Non-Direct Marketing Businesses by Dan S. Kennedy

Guerilla Marketing: Easy and Inexpensive Strategies for Making Big Profits from Your Small Business by Jay Conrad Levinson, Jeannie Levinson, and Amy Levinson

How to Write a Good Advertisement by Victor O. Schwab

Copywriting for Beginners: The Basic Steps on Producing the Best Copywriting for the Web by James Graham

Ultimate Guide to Facebook Advertising: How to Access 1 Billion Potential Customers in 10 Minutes (Ultimate series) by Perry Marshall, Keith Krance, and Thomas Meloche

Ultimate Guide to YouTube for Business (Ultimate series) by Jason R. Rich

Anxiety

If you have ever suffered from any kind of anxiety, this is going to be a life-saving list of books that will change and heal your life. These are must reads, as they will create in you the wisdom and ability to get out of the anxiety you are suffering. These have helped me live an amazing life, even after my life felt hopeless.

TLM The Linden Method: Be Who You Want to Be, by Charles Linden BA Hons

All is Well: Heal Your Body with Medicine, Affirmations, and Intuition by Louise Hay and Mona Lisa Schulz

How to Live 365 Days a Year by John A. Schindler

The Breath Bath: 4 Steps to Breathe Your Way to the Ultimate Makeover by Priya Narthakii

Striking Thoughts: Bruce Lee's Wisdom for Daily Living (Bruce Lee Library) by Bruce Lee and John Little

E-Squared: Nine Do-It-Yourself Energy Experiments that Prove Your Thoughts Create Your Reality by Pam Grout

The Relaxation Response by Herbert Benson and Miriam Z. Klipper

Peace Is Every Breath: A Practice for Our Busy Lives by Thich Nhat Hanh

Stress Free in 30 Days by Charles Linden

Battlefield of the Mind: Winning the Battle in Your Mind by Joyce Meyer

You Are the Placebo: Making Your Mind Matter by Dr. Joe Dispenza

Fearless Living: Live Without Excuses and Love Without Regret by Rhonda Britten

The Sedona Method: Your Key to Lasting Happiness, Success, Peace and Emotional Well-Being by Hale Dwoskin

Sales

We are all salesmen in some form or fashion. We all are selling ourselves on a daily basis. If you want to learn sales as a career, then this list of books can and will change your sales skills and propel you to the top of the mountain if you will implement them in your life. Sales success depends on knowing who your customer is and what their needs are to make sure you are offering them the best solutions to their problems.

Selling 101: What Every Successful Sales Professional Needs to Know by Zig Ziglar

The 25 Sales Habits of Highly Successful Salespeople by Stephan Schiffman

The Greatest Salesman in the World by Og Mandino

Persuade Anyone with NLP: A Teach Yourself Guide (Teach Yourself: General Reference) by Alice Muir

Convince Them in 90 Seconds or Less: Make Instant Connections that Pay Off in Business and in Life by Nicholas Boothman

The Ultimate Sales Machine: Turbocharge Your Business with Relentless Focus on 12 Key Strategies by Chet Holmes

The Art of Closing the Sale: The Key to Making More Money Faster in the World of Professional Selling by Brian Tracy

The Ultimate Sales Machine: Turbocharge Your Business with Relentless Focus on 12 Key Strategies by Chet Holmes

Power Verbs for Presenters: Hundreds of Verbs and Phrases to Pump Up Your Speeches and Presentations by Michael Lawrence Faulkner and Michelle Faulkner-Lunsford

Ziglar on Selling: The Ultimate Handbook for the Complete Sales Professional by Zig Ziglar

If You're Not First, You're Last: Sales Strategies to Dominate Your Market and Beat Your Competition by Grant Cardone

The Ultimate Sales Letter: Attract New Customers. Boost your Sales. by Dan S. Kennedy

No B.S. Sales Success in The New Economy by Dan S. Kennedy

No B.S. Guide to Brand-Building by Direct Response: The Ultimate No Holds Barred Plan to Creating and Profiting from a Powerful Brand Without Buying It by Dan S. Kennedy

The 250 Power Words That Sell: The Words You Need to Get the Sale, Beat Your Quota, and Boost Your Commission by Stephan Schiffman

The 10X Rule: The Only Difference Between Success and Failure by Grant Cardone

Getting to Yes: Negotiating Agreement Without Giving In by Roger Fisher, William L. Ury, and Bruce Patton

Integrity Selling: How to Succeed in Selling in the Competitive Years Ahead by R. Willingham

*The Ultimate Success Secret b*y Dan S. Kennedy

Zero Resistance Selling by Maxwell Maltz

Personal Development

This is a large list of personal development books that are in my personal library. These have and still change my life on a daily basis. Look through this list and see if you identify with anything you want to achieve in your own life and make sure you take the time to read some of these books.

Think and Grow Rich: The Landmark Bestseller by Napoleon Hill

The Think and Grow Rich Action Pack by Napoleon Hill

Notes from a Friend: A Quick and Simple Guide to Taking Charge of Your Life by Anthony Robbins

It Takes Respect by Aeneas Williams

The Warrior Ethos by Steven Pressfield

Positive Thinking Every Day: An Inspiration for Each Day of the Year by Dr. Norman Vincent Peale

The Return of the Ragpicker by Og Mandino

The Greatest Salesman in the World, Part 2: The End of the Story by Og Mandino

The Greatest Success in the World by Og Mandino

The Greatest Miracle in the World by Og Mandino

How to Develop Self-Confidence and Influence People by Public Speaking by Dale Carnegie

Secrets for Success and Happiness by Og Mandino

Butt Prints in the Sand—No More!: Make Footprints in Your Personal and Professional Life by Sam Glenn

The Master Key System by Charles F. Haanel

Power of Positive Living by Norman Vincent Peale

Three Feet from Gold: Turn Your Obstacles in Opportunities by Sharon L. Lechter and Greg S. Reid

Creating Affluence: The A-to-Z Steps to a Richer Life by Deepak Chopra

Man's Search for Meaning by Viktor E. Frankl

The Decision Book: 50 Models for Strategic Thinking by Mikael Krogerus and Roman Tschäppeler

Succeed and Grow Rich through Persuasion: Revised Edition by Napoleon Hill

As a Man Thinketh: Keepsake Edition by James Allen

John T. Molloy's New Dress for Success by John T. Molloy

The Ultimate Marketing Plan: Target Your Audience! Get Out Your Message! Build Your Brand! by Dan S. Kennedy

You Can Work Your Own Miracles by Napoleon Hill

Accelerated Learning for the 21st Century: The Six-Step Plan to Unlock Your Master-Mind by Colin Rose

The Success Principles: How to Get from Where You Are to Where You Want to Be
by Jack Canfield and Janet Switzer

The Authentic Swing: Notes from the Writing of a First Novel by Steven Pressfield

The Strangest Secret by Earl Nightingale

The Amazing Results of Positive Thinking by Dr. Norman Vincent Peale

The Power of Positive Thinking by Dr. Norman Vincent Peale

The Power of Habit: Why We Do What We Do in Life and Business by Charles Duhigg

Hero (The Secret) by Rhonda Byrne

Wake Up and Live! by Dorothea Brande

Napoleon Hill's Golden Rules: The Lost Writings by Napoleon Hill

Think and Grow Rich: Stickability, The Power of Perseverance by Greg S. Reid and The Napoleon Hill Foundation

The War of Art: Break Through the Blocks and Win Your Inner Creative Battles by Steven Pressfield

The Psychology of Winning by Denis Waitley

Goals!: How to Get Everything You Want Faster Than You Ever Thought Possible by Brian Tracy

Make Yourself Unforgettable: How to Become the Person Everyone Remembers and No One Can Resist by Dale Carnegie Training

Unlimited Power: The New Science of Personal Achievement by Anthony Robbins

Grow a Pair: How to Stop Being a Victim and Take Back Your Life, Your Business, and Your Sanity by Larry Winget

Turning Pro: Tap Your Inner Power and Create Your Life's Work by Steven Pressfield

Life Without Limits: Inspiration for a Ridiculously Good Life by Nick Vujicic

The Power of Intention by Dr. Wayne W. Dyer

Shut Up, Stop Whining, and Get a Life: A Kick-Butt Approach to a Better Life by Larry Winget

It Takes Respect by Aeneas Williams

7 Habits of Highly Effective People: Powerful Lessons in Personal Change by Stephen. R. Covey

Awaken the Giant Within: How to Take Immediate Control of Your Mental, Emotional, Physical and Financial Destiny! by Tony Robbins

Public Speaking for Success by Dale Carnegie

The Magic of Thinking Big by David J. Schwartz

Outliers: The Story of Success by Malcolm Gladwell

The Alchemist by Paulo Coelho

Influence: The Psychology of Persuasion, Revised Edition by Robert B. Cialdini

Ten Powerful Phrases for Positive People by Rich DeVos

The Shift: Taking Your Life from Ambition to Meaning by Dr. Dwayne W. Dyer

The Secret by Rhonda Byrne

The One Minute Millionaire: The Enlightened Way to Wealth by Mark Victor Hansen and Robert G. Allen

Breaking the Habit of Being Yourself: How to Lose Your Mind and Create a New One by Dr. Joe Dispenza
Enough is Enough!: Stop Enduring and Start Living Your Extraordinary Life by Jane Straus

30 Lessons for Living: Tried and True Advice from the Wisest Americans by Karl Pillemer

The Success System That Never Fails by William Clement Stone

Success Through A Positive Mental Attitude by Napoleon Hill and W. Stone

QBQ! The Question Behind the Question: Practicing Personal Accountability at Work and in Life by John G. Miller

Secrets of the Millionaire Mind: Mastering the Inner Game of Wealth by T. Harv Eker

How to Win Friends & Influence People by Dale Carnegie

10 Days to Faster Reading by The Princeton Language Institute and Abby Marks-Beale

Psycho-Cybernetics, A New Way to Get More Living Out of Life by Maxwell Maltz

NLP: The Essential Guide to Neuro-Linguistic Programming by NLP Comprehensive, Tom Dotz, Tom Hoobyar, and Susan Sanders

Spiritual Development

I am a youth pastor, and I believe in spiritual development as one of the most important parts of life. This does not mean you have to believe the way I do, but just keep an open mind to new things and you might just discover something that will change your life forever.

The Seven Spiritual Laws of Success: A Practical Guide to the Fulfillment of Your Dreams by Deepak Chopra

StrengthsFinder 2.0 by Tom Rath

The Road Home by Denise Jackson

You Changed My Life: Stories of Real People with Remarkable Hearts by Max Lucado

Grand Miracle by C.S. Lewis

Our Invisible Allies: The Definitive Guide on Angels and How They Work Behind the Scenes by Ron Phillips

Your Best Life Begins Each Morning: Devotions to Start Every New Day of the Year by Joel Osteen

Extraordinary Miracles in the Lives of Ordinary People: Inspiring Stories of Divine Intervention by Therese Marszalek

Live Like You Were Dying: A Story About Living by Michael Morris

The Seven Spiritual Laws for Parents: Guiding Your Children to Success and Fulfillment by Deepak Chopra

To Heaven and Back: A Doctor's Extraordinary Account of Her Death, Heaven, Angels, and Life Again: A True Story by Mary C. Neal

How to Stop Worrying and Start Living by Dale Carnegie

Proof of Heaven: A Neurosurgeon's Journey into the Afterlife by Eben Alexander III

Nearing Home: Life, Faith, and Finishing Well by Billy Graham

The Power of Now: A Guide to Spiritual Enlightenment by Eckhart Tolle

God Is Real: The Stunning New Convergence of Science and Spirituality by Sanjay C Patel

Viktor Frankl's Logotherapy: Method of Choice in Ecumenical Pastoral Psychology by Ann V. Graber

Manifest Your Destiny: The Nine Spiritual Principles for Getting Everything You Want by Wayne W. Dyer

No Death, No Fear: Comforting Wisdom for Life by Thich Nhat Hanh

Christianity According to the Bible: Separating Cultural Religion from Biblical Truth by Ron Rhodes

God Is in the Hard Stuff by Bruce Bickel and Stan Jantz

Stomping Out the Darkness: Discover Your True Identity in Christ and Stop Putting Up with the World's Garbage by Neil T. Anderson and Dave Park

The Purpose Driven Life by Rick Warren

Left to Tell: Discovering God Amidst the Rwandan Holocaust by Immaculee Ilibagiza

Your Best Life Now: 7 Steps to Living at Your Full Potential by Joel Osteen

Marriage and Relationships

These titles can be so important for you to take the time to read if you are married. Knowing that 50 percent of all marriages end in divorce, this stat alone should make you want to pick up a book on marriage to help you get it right so you don't become one of the negative statistics.

Don't Sweat the Small Stuff for Moms: Simple Ways to Stress Less and Enjoy Your Family More by Kristine Carlson

The 5 Love Languages: The Secret to Love That Lasts by Gary D Chapman

Married for Life: Inspirations from Those Married 50 Years or More by Bill Morelan

The Shelter of Each Other: Rebuilding Our Families by Mary Pipher

Traits of a Lasting Marriage by Jim Conway and Sally Conway

Love Life for Every Married Couple by Ed Wheat and Gloria Okes Perkins

Rekindling the Romance: Loving the Love of Your Life by Dennis Rainey and Barbara Rainey

How Can I Get Through to You?: Closing the Intimacy Gap Between Men and Women by Terrence Real

Relationship Breakthrough by Cloe Madanes ad Anthony Robbins

The Relationship Cure: A 5 Step Guide to Strengthening Your Marriage, Family, and Friendships by John Gottman

Why Marriages Succeed or Fail: And How You Can Make Yours Last by John Gottman

Uncommon Therapy: The Psychiatric Techniques of Milton H. Erickson, M.D. by Jay Haley

The Seven Principles for Making Marriage Work: A Practical Guide from the Country's Foremost Relationship Expert by John M. Gottman and Nan Silver

Behind the One-Way Mirror: Advances in the Practice of Strategic Therapy by Cloe Madanes

The Science of Trust: Emotional Attunement for Couples by John M. Gottman

*Marriage Fitness: 4 Steps to Building & Maintaining Phenomenal Love b*y Mort Fertel

Guide to Writing

The Essential Guide to Getting Your Book Published: How to Write It, and Market It . . . Successfully by Arielle Eckstut and David Henry Sterry

Audio Programs

For those of you who like to listen to books instead of reading them, these are the audio and DVD programs I have purchased over the years. Use your car as your learning vehicle—put a CD in every day while driving to make sure you are feeding your mind with the right food.

Sales

The Unfair Advantage: Sell With NLP! by Duane Lakin (Also available as a book.)

The Psychology of Selling: The Art of Closing Sales by Brian Tracy

Sell Like a Pro: How to Use Confidence, Enthusiasm and Influence for BIG Results by Dale Carnegie Training

Marketing

Piranha Marketing System (The Seven Success Multiplying Factors to Dominate Any Market You Enter) by Joe Polish

Personal Development

Accelerated Learning Techniques – The Express Track to Super Intelligence by Brian Tracy with Colin Rose

Lead the Field by Earl Nightingale

The Millionaire Messenger: Make a Difference and a Fortune Sharing Your Advice by Brendon Burchard

New Dynamics of Goal Setting: Flextactics for a Fast-Changing Future by Denis Waitley

The Miracle of Self-Discipline: The "No-Excuses" Way to Getting Things Done by Brian Tracy

Memory in a Month by Ron White

17 Principles of Success by Napoleon Hill

The New Psycho-Cybernectics: A Mind Technology for Living Your Life without Limits by Dr. Maxwell Maltz and Dan Kennedy

The Compound Effect by Darren Hardy

Theatre of the Mind: Creating Power and Results Through the Power of Mental Movies by Matt Furey

The Power Habits System: The New Science for Making Success Automatic by Noah St. John

Lessons in Mastery by Anthony Robbins

The Power to Shape your Destiny!: Seven Strategies for Massive Results by Anthony Robbins

Ultimate Edge by Anthony Robbins

Total Product Blueprint: The Unreleased Black Album by Brendon Burchard

Experts Academy by Brendon Burchard

The Teachings of Abraham: The Master Course CD by Esther and Jerry Hicks

Every Day a Friday: How to be Happier 7 days a week by Joel Osteen

Finished with Fear: Living Life with Confidence by Joel Osteen

Your Secret Wealth System by Jay Abraham

Challenge to Succeed by Jim Rohn

The Day That Turns Your Life Around: Remarkable Success Ideas that Can Change Your Life in an Instant by Jim Rohn and Darren Hardy

The Power of Ambition: Unleashing the Conquering Drive Within You by Jim Rohn

Cultivating an Unshakable Character: How to Walk Your Talk All the Way to the Top by Jim Rohn

The Weekend Seminar: Skills for the 21st Century by Jim Rohn

You Are the Placebo Mediation 1: Changing Two Beliefs and Perceptions by Dr. Joe Dispenza

You are the Placebo Mediation 2: Changing Two Beliefs and Perceptions by Dr. Joe Dispenza

Life Coaching

Core 100 DVD/CD Program Mastery Units 1-4: The New Standard for Human Change
by Robbins-Madanes Training

Business

How You Can Start, Build, Manage, or Turnaround Any Business by Brian Tracy

Success Mastery Academy: Reach Peak Levels of Performance in All Areas of Your Life by Brian Tracy

The Entrepreneurs Success Code by Jeff Burrows

Marriage and Relationships

"That's What I Was Going to Ask": Answers to the Most Common and Crucial Questions About Fixing Your Marriage by Mort Fertel

The Complete Marriage Fitness Workbook and Personal Journal by Mort Fertel

How would you like to become Extraordinary in any part of your life?

Eric is the President and founder of REAL Coaching & Consulting Group LLC

When you work with Eric he will bring his years of experience and expertise in both business and life to help you set and achieve your goals.

Author Speaker Coach

To schedule Eric to speak at your next event, meeting or training event, email me today at
REALCCG@GMAIL.COM

Or visit our website to learn more about what we can do for you.
http://www.realccg.com/

Do you want to be a better spouse? Do you want to have a better spouse?

If you answered yes to either of these questions, please contact me at the below email.

TheSmilingMarriage@gmail.com

AUTHOR SPEAKER COACH

Check out our website for some exciting information and programs.

www.TheSmilingMarriage.Com

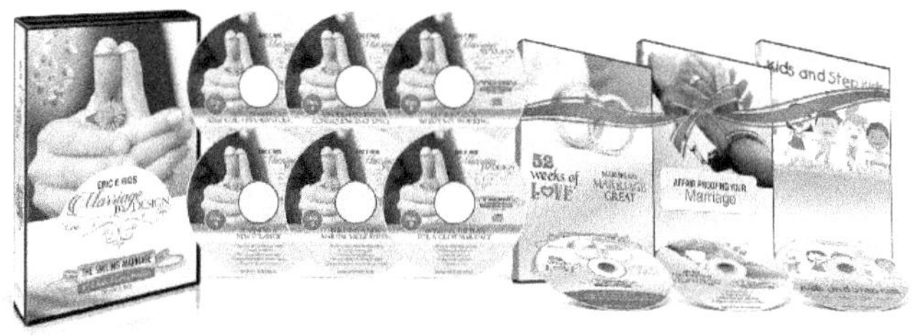

www.ingramcontent.com/pod-product-compliance
Lightning Source LLC
LaVergne TN
LVHW051057080426
835508LV00019B/1919
9780692478899